BEING A GIRL
Who Loves

Praise for *Being a Girl Who Loves*

"You have two choices when you are being tried by the unlovable people in your life. You can either scream or you can sing," says author Shannon Kubiak Primicerio. I love that! Shannon offers practical advice without beating around the bush. She's straightforward, genuine, and definitely passionate about helping teen girls become all God dreams for them.

Susie Shellenberger, *Editor of BRIO Magazine.*

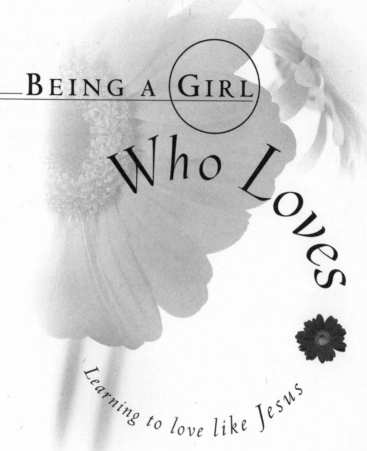

BEING A GIRL

Who Loves

Learning to love like Jesus

SHANNON KUBIAK
PRIMICERIO

BETHANYHOUSE
MINNEAPOLIS, MINNESOTA

Published by Bethany House Publishers
11400 Hampshire Avenue South
Bloomington, Minnesota 55438

Bethany House Publishers is a division of
Baker Publishing Group, Grand Rapids, Michigan.

Printed in the United States of America

Library of Congress Cataloging-in-Publication Data

Primicerio, Shannon Kubiak.
    Being a girl who loves : learning to love like Jesus / Shannon Kubiak Primicerio.
        p. cm. —(Being a girl)
    Summary: "Ideal for a girl's personal quiet time or for use in small groups, this book
offers practical insights into geing a girl who loves as Jesus loves"—Provided by publisher.
    ISBN 0-7642-0089-5 (pbk.)
    1. Teenage girls—Religious life—Juvenile literature. 2. Christian teenagers—Religious
life—Juvenile literature. I. Title II. Series:
    Primicerio, Shannon Kubiak. Being a Girl.

    BV4551.3.P75 2005
    248.8'33—dc22
                                                                    2005018682

To my husband, Michael:
I fall more in love with you every day.

About the Author

Twenty-something author Shannon Kubiak Primicerio is a recent bride who resides in Southern California with her husband, Michael. The Primicerios are a fun-loving couple who enjoy watching baseball, playing Bocce Ball, flying kites, and hanging out at the beach.

Shannon and Michael have a heart to see God glorified among youth. Together the two seek to offer practical applications to deep spiritual truths through a ministry of writing and speaking.

Shannon has a B.A. in Journalism and a minor in Biblical Studies from Biola University, and was the recipient of the *North County Times* "Excellence in Writing" award in 2000, and the San Diego Christian Writer's Guild "Nancy Bayless Award for Excellence in Writing" in 2003.

She has been interviewed on radio and television programs across the nation and was recently featured in such media outlets as PBS's *Religion and Ethics Newsweekly* and *Time* magazine.

Shannon's ministry spans the nations, as her books are available in several different languages. Her other books include *The Divine Dance* and *God Called a Girl*.

To learn more about Shannon, or to book her for an event, you can visit her at her Web site, *www.shannonkubiak.com*, or you can e-mail her at *shannon@shannonkubiak.com*. She loves hearing from her readers and seeks to answer all of her e-mail personally.

Contents

What Is Love?

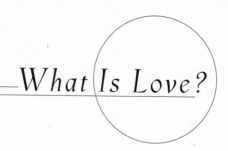

God is missing. Just watch five minutes of the evening news. We live in a world filled with evil and hate. Society is rapidly being destroyed by people who claim they do not need God, but what they don't realize is that rejecting God means rejecting *love*. In a world where "all faiths are created equal," people attempt to make God whatever they want Him to be— and in turn, they make love whatever they want it to be.

A well-known writer once said, "Love is the irresistible desire to be irresistibly desired." Most of us live as if we believe that is true. I initially thought it was a good definition—until I realized how selfish it is. No wonder we are missing the mark. It should be no surprise that God has gone missing from today's dreary world. We have abandoned everything we know to be true about love, and we have made it about us.

We are all out for ourselves. Like greedy monsters, we thrust our forceful fists into the hearts of everyone we meet, demanding that they give us love and take little in return. We want and we have, yet we are always left wanting. More than we want to love, we want to be loved. More than wanting to give and sacrifice, we want to be given to and sacrificed for. Somewhere along the line we have come to believe that we are worth something *just because*, yet others must prove their worth to us.

Close examination shows we do not even know what love is. We say, "I love pizza" and "I love my dog," then we turn around and say, "I love my family" and "I love God." How can one word accurately describe our feelings for all of those things? I mean, if we love pizza yet we will throw a leftover piece in the garbage, how does that translate when we say we love our friends? We have been misusing the term, and the true definition of love has been lost somewhere in translation.

What is love, anyway? First John 4:8 tells us that God is love. That means the cure for a world where love is missing is to fill it with God. The nature and acts of God are characterized by love. Love is the driving motivation behind all God does. You cannot have God without having love, because God himself is love and He cannot go against His own nature. Yes, John was right. God is love. And our world needs Him now more than ever before.

Pretend for a moment you are one of the lepers, or the paralytic, or the hemorrhaging woman Jesus healed. Close your eyes and imagine what it must have been like to be the thief on the cross next to Jesus who was promised paradise in his last hour.

What would the evening news be like tonight if it were filled with stories of triumph like that instead of the grim pictures of evil and defeat that we see filling our television screens each night? Love is a powerful thing, and in a world like ours, real love *always* stands out.

It is seen in the girl who befriends the new girl in school who dresses differently and talks a little funny. Glimpses can be caught in the girl who holds fast to hope and refuses to sleep with her boyfriend because she knows God created sex for the lasting union of marriage. Love reigns in the girl who obeys her parents when she doesn't exactly understand or agree with their rules. God smiles at the girl who demonstrates love by forgiving someone who has hurt her. And heaven explodes in monstrous applause at the sight of the girl whose heart is fully committed to Jesus.

Oh, how often we fall short. God has placed a beautiful song in our hearts, but we sing different lyrics. We were designed to love and be loved in a selfless way, yet we exhaust ourselves with efforts to make love something other than what God created it to be. It is about others, but we want so desperately to make it about us.

As Christians we can recite verses like John 3:16 from memory: "For God so loved the world..." and 1 Corinthians 13:4, which states, "Love is patient, love is kind." We can probably even hum the melody to Sunday school songs like,

"They will know we are Christians by our love, by our love...." But do we *live* like we believe those things? Do we love like we know what we are doing?

I am not talking *pepperoni-pizza-that-you-throw-into-the-trash-can* love. The love I am talking about is not *remembering-to-feed-your-dog-named-Floppy* kind of love. It's the *what-can-I-do-for-someone-else-today* kind of love that will grab the world with force and change it.

But Shannon, you might be thinking, *I am just one person. I can't change the world.* One person is all it takes. Just as God placed the strength of a leader in Moses, the heart of a shepherd king in David, the grace to be queen in Esther, and the heart of a servant in Jesus, God placed His love in you.

Multitudes everywhere are pushing and shoving each other—they don't stand out. It will be the one who walks through the multitudes quietly while gently loving others that will captivate the crowd. True love does not demand recognition for what it is doing. The reward of love is the joy it brings to the one it loves.

In second grade my teacher told my mom that during free time I was always walking around looking for the outcast, bringing them into a group and making sure they felt at home before moving on to someone else. Little did he know I did that only because I always feared that one day *I* would be the outcast, desperately wanting someone to take the time to draw me into the circle with everyone else. I longed to help others find their place in an attempt to find my place there as well.

Perhaps you are the girl who has never been invited into the circle. If you are, I am so sorry. No one should have to experience that. But now is your moment to shine. Now is your moment to find others who have spent their entire lives on the outside, and reach out to them with the compassionate love of Jesus Christ and make them feel at home.

For a while I regularly met with a girl who was having trouble with friends at school. The popular girls were only nice on certain days of the week, and every few days they went looking for someone to pick on, someone to reject, and someone to ridicule, just for fun. Their target was usually my friend. Finally one day I asked her about the other girls in her class.

"Oh, they're really nice," she said, "just not as popular." Gently I reminded her how awful she felt when she was left out or went unnoticed by those around her. Then I began to explain how the less popular girls must have felt if no one ever wanted to be their friend, just because they weren't as well known around campus.

Eventually she saw my point—and her opportunity. Knowing the depths of her own hurting heart, my friend reached out in kindness to these other girls. They began writing each other notes, hanging out after school, and doing group projects together. And the strangest thing happened: My friend forgot all about the popular girls who hurt her. She made real friends who stuck up for her and stood by her.

One day the popular girls noticed what had happened and

began to sweet-talk my friend, inviting her back into their circle. If all of the other girls in the class wanted to be her friend, these girls certainly did too. My friend surprised them though. She was nice to them in response to their offer, but she never rejoined their clique. Feeling rejected, the popular girls decided to hurl insults at her and spread rumors about her around school.

But my friend no longer cared. She had taken the power away from those who hurt her, and she reached out and made some new—true—friends. Sometimes being the one who is pushed out of the circle is just part of God's plan to get you to reach out to those not in your circle.

If you are the girl who has always been on the inside, now is your chance to offer the acceptance you have received to someone who desperately needs it. Look beyond your circle for a minute, and reach out to those who are in desperate need of love. Maybe it will cost you something in terms of acceptance or comfort to reach out, but do for others what you would want them to do for you. After all, you never know when you are going to find yourself on the outside of the "in crowd." Sometimes when we refuse to step out, God will allow us to be pushed out. Trust me, it's always less painful when we *choose* to reach out to others.

Maybe you know what it's like to be on both sides of the circle—you have been welcomed in, and you have been left out. Then you know better than anyone out there just how good it feels to be loved, and how horrible it is to be unloved.

Your compassion meter should be well-tuned as you set out to seek those who are in desperate need of a friend.

In college I met a very beautiful and popular girl who was always reaching out to others. We'll call her Kim. She had long blond hair, perfectly tanned skin, a bright white smile, and dark brown eyes that were known to melt many of the male hearts around campus. I always knew of her, but I didn't really get to know her until my last semester. We were assigned to the same group in a class, and we had to share our life stories.

When Kim's turn came, I was shocked as she tearfully shared about her junior high and high school days. A self-described loner, the now beautiful and popular Kim used to eat lunch alone, locked in a bathroom stall where others couldn't see that she was by herself. Suddenly I understood why Kim was always reaching out to the underdog. I saw why she was making sure the freshmen felt welcomed and the loners felt included. And I came to respect Kim more in that moment, as she sat in a pool of her own tears, than I ever had before.

The world needs more people like Kim. Ever since that fall afternoon when we sat under the trees and watched the leaves turn as we talked about our lives, I have tried to be more like her. And I have been eternally grateful for all of the Kims I have met in my life, when I desperately needed someone to open her heart, offer her hand, and show me the way.

That's what Jesus meant when He told His disciples that

the world will know we are Christians by our love for one another. It's what Paul meant when he told Timothy we are to be an example in our love. It's what Jesus meant when He said we are to love like He loved.

Love is what makes us different. Love is everything. It's not too late to change the world. It only takes one person to spark a great movement. You are that one. I am that one.

But we have a choice: We can love, or we can refuse to love. We can embrace God and His love, or we can reject Him completely. There is no middle ground. First John 4:7–8 says one who does not love does not know God. Your actions are speaking louder than your words.

This isn't a book that was written to be read in one sitting. Each chapter focuses on one aspect of love and offers both scriptural counsel and practical advice on how to live that principle out in your life. Spend time in each chapter— answer the questions at the end by writing them in your journal, discussing them in a small group, or sharing with a friend. Put love into action with the suggested activity. Focus on the theme of one chapter until you think you're getting the hang of it, and *then* move onto the next. When you are done with the book, come back to it every now and then to check your progress. None of us can become a girl who loves genuinely and truly overnight. It takes time spent in prayer and fellowship with God to learn to love as He does.

We can either be girls of this world, or girls of God. I don't know about you, but in the end I want to come out being a girl who loves.

1

As I Have Loved You

Imagine with me for a minute that you are dating the most wonderful guy in the entire world. He's tall, good-looking, sensitive, and yet strong—for the sake of this illustration let's just say he is perfect. Pretend it's your birthday. He has the "world's best date" planned, and you have been excited about it for weeks. You get all dolled up in your finest outfit—your hair is perfect, your makeup is flawless. And you even turn down dinner at your favorite restaurant with your parents so you can go out on this big birthday date.

But when Mr. Wonderful finally calls you, your smile quickly drops and your high hopes come crashing to the ground only to catch on fire and evaporate completely. Not only is he half an hour late, but he is asking *you* to come pick *him* up. Feeling as if you have no other choice, you oblige. When you arrive, his stereo is blaring so loudly you have to pound on his door for ten whole minutes before he answers.

Finally he comes to the door in his dirty, smelly workout clothes and hops in your passenger's seat (without even complimenting you on how you look). He looks at you with a charming smile and says, "So where we goin'?" Relieved that you get to pick, yet embarrassed by the way he is dressed, you suggest your favorite place to eat.

Wiping the back of his hand across his sweaty brow, he makes a face and says, "Naw. I was thinking more of something like Burger Barn."

Refusing to argue, you go along with his plan—only to find out he expects *you* to pay. Now, this story could go on forever, but I think you get the point. There's nothing wonderful about someone who has no regard for anyone else. Perhaps the big birthday date *was* Mr. Wonderful's idea of a great date, since he was getting a free meal and being chauffeured around town. But the truth is, nobody can have an ideal time with someone who thinks life is all about him.

As extreme as my example may be, we all tend to have our moments when we behave like Mr. Not-So-Wonderful. We walk around as if we are God's gift to our friends and family, and we act as if we reside in a universe in which we are the center. With no regard for others and their feelings, we do what it takes to get what we want, no matter what it costs those around us.

Instead of loving others, we spend our efforts on loving ourselves. We operate with an *It's all about me* mentality, not realizing how ugly it makes us. And not only that, when we behave in a selfish, glory-seeking manner, we break the heart of our loving God, who sacrificed His all just to be with us.

We live as if we believe God said, "Love yourself with all

your heart and expect others to love you just as ꭒ
on earth did we get this idea? That's just d
always seem to notice how repulsive it is in otl
was the last time we closely examined ourselves?

IT'S NOT ABOUT YOU

In 1 Corinthians 13:4–8 the apostle Paul describes it this
way:

> Love is patient, love is kind, and is not jealous; love
> does not brag and is not arrogant, does not act unbe-
> comingly; it does not seek its own, is not provoked, does
> not take into account a wrong suffered, does not rejoice
> in unrighteousness, but rejoices with the truth; bears all
> things, believes all things, hopes all things, endures all
> things. Love never fails.

I have been told many times that we can test how loving
we are by inserting our name in place of the word "love" in
the above passage. I would flunk on the first try: "Shannon
is patient." No, I'm really not—especially not *all* the time.
How about you? How would you rate if you had to judge
yourself by that standard? Chances are you would probably
rank somewhere near me in the not-very-loving category. In
an attempt to work on this, my friend Hana picks out one
characteristic of love to focus on each day. At the end of the
day she journals what she learned as a way of charting her

growth. It's been a great thing for her, and it may be for you as well.

If love is not about us, many times we are left wondering who—or what—it is about. Simply put, love is not about the one loving but about the one *being loved*. If we all operated under this mentality all the time, the world would be a perfect place. We would be thinking of others and they would be thinking of us, and everyone's needs would be met.

Unfortunately, though, the world is not a perfect place. Instead of thinking of others, we all walk around demanding our own rights and dictating what is fair and not fair in light of how our own needs are or aren't being met. How on earth did we get so far off course? What have we done with Jesus' command to love as He loved us?

The downward spiral of man's demise was set in motion when Eve first ate the forbidden fruit back in Eden because she wanted to be just like God. The problem started when Eve wanted what was best for Eve with no regard for what it would do to God's plan, Adam, and the entire world.

Our problem starts in much the same manner. We want to date the popular guy, so we chase him, ignoring the fact that he has a girlfriend. We want to be voted prom queen, so we talk poorly about the other girls who are running in order to get the votes that would have gone to them. We want people to like us, so we talk down to others in the group to make ourselves look and feel superior. Do you see the problem with these statements? They all begin with the words *we want*.

Now, wanting something in and of itself is not always a bad thing. But why do we want? How do we want? And what is that want doing to us? Sometimes we can want love too much, and like green-eyed monsters, we are consumed by our desire as we try to take hold of love with no regard for anyone else.

THERE'S NO SUCH THING AS MANIPULATIVE LOVE

I once knew a girl who would give, give, and give in an attempt to become the "super friend." But she used her giving as an excuse for demanding from her friends whatever she wanted. It went something like this:

I bought you this really cute and expensive shirt at the mall, remember? By the way, I need a ride to the football game. I know you weren't planning on going, but you're really my only hope and it's important to me.

Most people responded by taking the shirt and giving the ride—even if complaining inwardly the entire time. Eventually, though, most people refused the gifts and didn't give the rides. No one likes to be manipulated. Manipulation is not love—it is a twisted version of a good thing. Love is giving *without* expecting something in return; it's not giving out of guilt or mixed motives.

Manipulation is seen in the temptation of Jesus found in Matthew 4:8–9. Satan takes Jesus to the top of a mountain and shows Him all the kingdoms of the world and their glory. Can't you just see the evil sneer painted across his ugly face as he showed Jesus what he had done to a once perfect world? Jesus must have winced in pain at the suffering He inventoried while standing there. I can hear Him thinking, *It wasn't supposed to be like this.*

Satan played on Jesus' heartstrings and then said, "All these things I will give You, if You fall down and worship me" (v. 9). Praise God we serve a Lord who cannot be manipulated. Although Jesus saw the pain and suffering of the current world, He would not immediately end it by giving in to Satan's self-gratifying desires. What good would have come of that? When we love we become more like God; when we manipulate we become like the devil himself.

Manipulation is selfishness trying to disguise itself as love.

No good ever comes from manipulating another, or from being manipulated by someone you love. Manipulation is selfishness trying to disguise itself as love. Beware: It is something we can all fall into a little too naturally. We should do regular motive checks to make sure our best efforts are really coming forth out of love and not manipulation.

We should also make sure we are not being manipulated by others. If you have a closet full of "free" shirts from a friend, for example, you might want to ask yourself what you really "paid" for those shirts. Did you have to do something to earn your friend's friendship and favor? Did she manipulate you into doing something you didn't really want to do? If so, it may be time to invite your friend over and have a little chat.

TWO KINDS OF LOVE

In the end there are two kinds of true love. There is gentle love and tough love. Both are needed for survival. And both are exemplified in God himself.

Gentle love is the side of God that sent Jesus to die in our place—it is self-sacrificing and nurturing, a warm and welcoming kind of love. This is the type of love we all crave so desperately. Tough love is the side of God that says no one can enter the gates of heaven except those who come through Jesus Christ. Salvation is offered to all but is only given to those who accept it on God's terms.

Those who did not accept Jesus while on earth will not be able to buy their way into heaven someday. Can't you just see someone trying to pay God off at the pearly gates? *Hey, God. I'll give you my field-level seats at the World Series if you let me into heaven.* As if God has not been to every World Series game ever played anyway.

There will not be scalpers lining the streets of gold, trying to sell last-minute tickets into heaven to anyone who missed his or her chance while on earth. Salvation does not work that way. Grace is balanced with justice and enforced with tough love.

One of the hardest things to learn about love is where to

find the balance between the tough and the gentle side. Gentle love would be forgiving your best friend for hurting your feelings when she blew you off to go and do something else. Tough love would be confronting your friend when this happens repeatedly. Love is not about you, but it doesn't mean you should be a doormat either.

In the end you need to ask, "What is best for my friend in this situation?" *and* "What is best for me in this situation?" Asking only one of those questions makes you either a punching bag or a self-centered creep. In the above example, if confronting your friend does not work, the best thing for both of you would be to go your separate ways. In Acts 15:39–41 Paul and Barnabas had a "sharp disagreement" and chose to take different paths. The end result was a blessing for both of them. Love is not always sticking together no matter what. True love knows when to hold on and when to let go.

Now, I am not saying we should drop our friends and move on to someone new as soon as we are mistreated. We live with *imperfect* people. And we need to realize that hurt is just part of life in a world filled with sin. The types of friends we may need to walk away from are those who tend to be abusive, manipulative, and vengeful on a regular basis. This does not include those who tend to be mean or selfish every once in a while—we all do that. But when a friendship starts to threaten who you are or what you believe, and you feel pressured to do things you don't want to do, then it is time to walk away.

Learning the Balance

True love is about giving *and* taking. It's about being needed *and* needing others. You can't do just one or the other. True love demands a balance of both. God created us to need community. In Genesis 2:18 God himself says it is not good for man to be alone.

Sometimes true love is seen in giving people some space, getting up and walking away, or in accepting the fact that growing up sometimes means growing apart from some of our friends. Other times it is seen in standing side by side through all seasons of life. Looking back through my life I see that different time periods were marked by different groups of friends.

Certain people have been there for every season of my life. But most of my friends from other seasons are not people I see regularly—or at all—anymore. That does not mean the memories are not great, and it does not mean I never loved them when they were actively part of my life. But then I look at certain members of my extended family and I realize I can't escape them. Matter of fact, I'll never be able to lose contact with them. So loving them means enduring them and offering grace in place of anger or revenge.

Sometimes the best thing you can do for a friend is to *be there* for her—let her cry on your shoulder when her heart is broken. Recently a friend of mine, we'll call him Rick, was telling me that our friend, who we'll call Steve, called him in tears. Before Steve could even choke out what happened, Rick told him he would drive down and meet him so they could talk in person. That response is a good example of gentle love in action.

Gentle love does not work in every situation, but we should always try it first. When we feel as if we are being manipulated or taken advantage of, tough love comes into play. It's not about always winning in the end, or getting what you want out of the situation. Love is about doing what is best for the other person. Sometimes that is giving them what they *want*; other times it is giving them what they *need*.

Tough love is needed for the girl whose boyfriend keeps pressuring her to have sex, or drink alcohol, or do anything she does not feel comfortable doing. No matter how much she loves him, breaking up is necessary for obvious reasons in that situation. She would not be loving her boyfriend or respecting herself by staying in the relationship; instead, she would be putting them both in harm's way by staying in a tempting and dangerous situation.

No wonder the first thing on Paul's list of love's characteristics was patience. When we are trying to learn the balance between gentle love and tough love, a lot of patience is required. In high school some of my Christian friends (guys and girls) and I befriended a group of non-Christian guys in a local band. We all went to the same school, and we hung out in the same places around town. My friends and I modeled our faith with our lives, and we made sure these guys always understood there was an open invitation to come to youth group with us.

We would openly discuss our beliefs *and their beliefs* without forcing our faith on them or putting them in a threatening environment. We never attacked them or made them feel backed into a corner. Last time I heard, five of those six guys had come to Christ. Sometimes patience is the key that unlocks a door for you, enabling you to pour God's love into a hurting heart. I think the "microwave mentality" of our generation has wrongly convinced us that results should always be instant.

LOOKING FOR THOSE TO LOVE

Many times in ministering to those around us we need to start with plain and simple encouragement. When Jesus first called His disciples, He went to the unlikely and unlovable. He made them extraordinary men by calling forth the gifts He saw in each of them.

Sometimes our gifts, talents, and passions are the very tools God uses to help us come alongside others and pour out God's love on them. I spoke at a public high school Career Day not long ago. While there I met a boy who was an outspoken agnostic. His rude comments annoyed his peers and even began to frustrate me. But I heard God's still, small voice whisper: *Love him.* What? Where is the logic in that?

But I did it anyway. When I left campus that day, Jimmy, as we'll call him, asked for my e-mail address so he could get some advice on writing. And of the hundreds of kids who met me and took my business card that afternoon, Jimmy was the only one who actually e-mailed me. First his e-mails were just about writing and how to get published. He had potential, so I always pointed out his strong points before making suggestions about improving other things.

The more he wrote, the more I saw that Jimmy was hurting. He felt unloved and unpopular, and his dark personality and rude comments were his way of protecting himself. So I always wrote back with a compliment on his writing, and even though I knew he was an agnostic, I didn't hesitate to write verses or other Christian thoughts at the end of my e-mails when led by the Lord to do so.

Eventually Jimmy came to me for advice on life, and when I asked if he would be interested in meeting a youth leader friend of mine and talking about God, Jimmy eagerly accepted. For me, being an author opened a door in the heart of an agnostic boy who hardened himself to everyone around him. In time, my kindness wore Jimmy's wall down, and he began to ask about God. Yes, love is patient and it is kind. And people *always* notice—even when you think they don't. Do you have any Jimmys in your life?

In high school I was a checker at a local craft store. Sometimes my line would wrap around half the store, and as a result irritated customers would usually pelt me with rude remarks as I rang up their purchases. But there was always one person who would come to me with a warm smile and shower me with kindness. At the end of the day, *that* was the person I always remembered. They were like a fresh drink of cool water on a hot day in the desert. Who do you know that could use a drink today?

What did Jesus mean when He said, "Love as I have loved you"? He meant love those like Judas who will betray you, love those like Peter whose love is imperfect and faltering, and love those like Mary Magdalene who have an ugly past. But even more than that, He meant love unselfishly and unreservedly. Love with reckless abandon.

No nail was strong enough to keep the King of the world hanging on a Roman cross while being mocked and criticized. Love was the only thing that could do that. When God looked down from heaven and saw Jesus being scourged and taunted and spit on, don't you think He wanted to reach down and stop it? He most certainly did! But His love for you and me prevented Him from doing that. Do we love Him with the same fervor?

Do we love Him like He loves us? We serve a Lord who died for us—but do we truly live for Him? And do we love His people with a love so patient, kind, and nonjudgmental that they take notice?

In Romans 5:8 Paul tells us, "God demonstrates His own love toward us, in that while we were yet sinners, Christ died for us." It's just like that old saying goes: "Love the sinner, hate the sin." That's how we are to love. We are to love people as they are, yet strive to build into their lives in order to make them better. Now don't misunderstand what I am saying and read this to say we are to try to *change* people. That's not our job—ever. That's God's job. We are simply to love people where they are at, and extend an encouraging hand to them as we help them along their journey.

Think of the people right now who have extended their love to you. Have you thanked them lately? Have you let them know how grateful you are that they came to you with a heart like Christ's and *chose* to love you?

Love is always a choice.

Love is always a choice. It's not a feeling. I've heard people say, "I can't help it if I'm not in love with him." I agree that when you fall in love with someone, there are a lot of factors that come into play, but I am not talking about being *in love* with someone. I am simply talking about *loving* someone. I am talking about building relationships with imperfect people by using the love of a perfect God.

A SUPERNATURAL THING

As we continue to journey together through this book, we will cover many aspects of love, including how we demonstrate it in the context of various relationships, and why we even love at all. But before we ever get to all of that, it is important that we understand *love is a supernatural thing*. If we rely on our own heart, we will always fail miserably.

On our own we are not capable of self-sacrificing love, just as we are not capable of producing ESPN by strapping an antenna to our head. In order to produce cable stations on our

TVs, we have to be plugged into the cable source. In the same way, in order to produce genuine love, we must be plugged into the source of love himself—God. We need to be plugged into Him through prayer, regular reading of His Word, and obedience to what He says. In a sense, our responsibility is like that of a wife whose husband is going away on a long business trip.

"Love the children for me," he says as he kisses her goodbye.

"And how shall I do that?" Her face is scrunched up in confusion as she looks at the man who has treated her as a true princess since day one.

"That's easy," her ever-patient husband replies. "Love them as I have loved you."

The very Lover of our souls has lavished love's richest blessings upon us, and He has asked us to do the same. We are to love Him and love others with a love so powerful it moves heaven and earth. So as you bask in the goodness of the love Christ has bestowed on you, don't just sit there—go out and share it with others.

Love them as He has loved you.

FOR FURTHER THOUGHT:

1. Have you ever known anyone who lived as if life was all about them? How did being around them make you feel?

2. Do you have a tendency to live life like it is all about you? Why or why not?

3. Have you ever been manipulated by someone you love? How did it make you feel?

4. What are some ways you use manipulation as a tool for your gain?

5. What are some practical ways you can love others the way Christ loves you?

LOVE IN ACTION:

Spend the next twenty-four hours paying close attention to how you interact with those you love. Make a list of things you do well (e.g., take time to help others when they need it) and a list of things you need to work on (e.g., get frustrated easily with those who don't meet *my* needs). Then stick the list in your Bible, or someplace you will see it, and make a conscious effort to become even more loving than you already are. Remember, true love is a supernatural thing. You will not be able to do it in your own strength. So pray and ask God to give you His love for the people around you. Use Christ's love as the standard. How can you love others the way He loves you?

2

It's the Greatest

In all honesty I would have blown right by her. My husband (who at the time was still just my boyfriend) had arrived back in the United States a mere two hours before we met Patty. And after nearly four months apart, the last thing I wanted to do was spend time with anyone but Michael. It was already hard enough that I had to say good-bye to him a few hours later so I could go teach a girls' Bible study. Four hours of seeing him just wasn't enough! He had been abroad finishing Bible college, and the separation had worn on both of us.

After one hundred and ten days of being apart, long e-mails, and static-ridden international cell phone calls, all I wanted to do was look the man I loved in the face, feel his arm wrapped tightly around my shoulders, and have a deep heart-to-heart conversation. God had other plans though.

I got out of the car and didn't even notice Patty at first. But Michael spotted her. He always notices people like Patty. Much like Jesus, he has an incredible ability to see those in need. In broken English she asked us if we wanted to purchase any of the items she had in her shopping cart.

She pulled out a bottle of barbeque sauce and a box of

macaroni and cheese. Patty made a concerted effort to convince us that each item was well worth the dollar she was charging for it. I considered giving her a dollar and sending her on her way, although I am not sure if I would have even done that had Michael not stopped. Surveying her frayed clothing, her sweaty brow, and her frail frame, he gave Patty his full attention.

"Are you hungry?" His voice was sincere, and he reached for my hand as he spoke to her.

"No speak English any good," she said, and tried to sell us the barbeque sauce again.

"Do you speak Spanish?" Neither Michael nor I speak any Spanish, but I am sure he would have found someone who could. But Patty told us she was from Iran and spoke Farsi. We really had no way of communicating with her. But Michael tried again.

"Would you like some food?" He pointed to the Carl's Jr. sign, and she began to catch on. As he went inside to buy her a meal, I sat outside with her as she stood guard over her shopping cart and told me as much of her story as she could in broken English. I could tell it had been quite some time since anyone had asked Patty about her life.

She was an eighty-year-old immigrant who had lost her son to cancer after coming to the States with him. She had no money, no real income, and could not afford to go back home. The sadness and deep sense of loss in her eyes was almost overwhelming. I had no idea what I could do to help. So I simply listened to her and let her talk. When Michael returned with the food, he asked her a simple question.

"Patty, have you ever read the Bible?" She nodded and told us she had a copy in her native tongue. Suddenly her eyes lit up with understanding.

"Are you Christians?" Her question came through a mouth full of food. I nodded enthusiastically.

"Yes, are you?" There was excitement in my voice as I answered. Her eyes grew a little dim before answering.

"No," she said softly as she chewed her French fries. "I'm a Muslim."

My heart sank, but Michael was undeterred. Without batting an eye he began to tell Patty the story of John and Peter found in Acts 3. As he talked with Patty that afternoon I came to a deeper understanding of what love is, and how truly *great* love is when it is shared.

Acts 3:1–8 says:

> Now Peter and John were going up to the temple at the ninth hour, the hour of prayer. And a certain man who had been lame from his mother's womb was being carried along, whom they used to set down every day at the gate of the temple which is called Beautiful, in order to beg alms of those who were entering the temple.
>
> And when he saw Peter and John about to go into the temple, he began asking to receive alms. And Peter, along with John, fixed his gaze upon him and said, "Look at us!"

And he began to give them his attention, expecting to receive something from them.

But Peter said, "I do not possess silver and gold, but what I do have I give to you: In the name of Jesus Christ the Nazarene—walk!"

And seizing him by the right hand, he raised him up; and immediately his feet and ankles were strengthened. And with a leap, he stood upright and began to walk; and he entered the temple with them, walking and leaping and praising God.

Michael's words to Patty that day were close to Peter's words to the beggar.

"Patty," he said gently, hesitating only slightly. "We're young and we don't have a lot of money and we are getting married soon, so we cannot give you any money today. But we can give you a warm meal, and we can tell you that Jesus loves you and that He wants to take care of you if you will come to Him."

"Thank you for taking time for me today."

There was no radical conversion in the parking lot that afternoon. In fact, after Patty finished eating she quickly went on her way to continue attempting to sell her groceries for double what she got them for. But before she left I will never forget what she said to me. In her thick accent she turned and looked both Michael and me in the eye and said,

"Thank you for taking time for me today."

I think our time was even more valuable to her than the meal we bought her. To her, our time was equivalent to love, and love was something it was evident Patty did not have a lot of in her life. To Patty, our time was the greatest gift we could have given her that afternoon. She showed her appreciation by offering some sort of Iranian blessing over us as she left.

Only hours later did I realize the magnitude of what we had done for her. And it was only then that I heard the voice of the Lord whisper, *Whatever you do unto the least of these you do unto Me.*

Much like the man Peter and John encountered at the temple gate, Patty was looking for money on the November afternoon we met her. Instead, both Patty and the beggar received something greater—love, compassion, and at least a little bit of Jesus. Our love toward Patty caused her to recognize right away that we were Christians.

IT'S A POWERFUL THING

Love is a powerful thing, and often it is far more powerful than we realize. First Corinthians 13:13 tells us that three things abide: faith, hope, and love. But it also tells us, "The greatest of these is love." It's hard to imagine anything being greater than faith and hope.

Faith is what keeps you going when the road is dark and you cannot see the way. It's what you lean on when all of your plans are coming unraveled and your heart is ready to burst.

Hope is what helps you survive when you are burying your dead dreams and you seemingly have nothing left.

Love, though, is greater than both faith and hope because it lets you know that no matter how rough life gets, you are not alone. It comes in simple yet meaningful forms. For Patty it was a simple meal and a half hour or so of conversation. For the beggar at the temple gate it was healing a lifelong infirmity. For the thief who hung next to Jesus on the cross, it was salvation in his last hour (Luke 23:39–43).

Imagine that. There he hung, a criminal fully deserving his penalty. He was a thief, a convict, a lowlife. Yet he spent his final hours hanging next to God himself. It was the perfect paradox—perfection hanging next to filth. Jesus had no reason to associate with this man. After all, Jesus was taking the sins of the world upon himself. There was no need to stop and converse with just one man—an evil and wicked man at that. Yet Jesus turned and looked at this man and said, "Today you shall be with Me in Paradise" (v. 43).

He didn't just give this man five minutes. He gave him eternity. He gave him the greatest thing He could have ever possibly given him. Forget about faith and hope—Jesus gave this man love. Freely and graciously Jesus heaped unmerited favor and love upon this wretched man. Perhaps that's what makes love so great. It isn't earned—at least not if it's real.

Jesus was not busy loving those who were busy loving themselves. Instead, He was busy loving those who had no one to love them. There are countless stories like the invalid, the leper, and the blind man. Many times we overlook these stories. We simply see that He brought them healing; we don't see that He first brought them love. Love is usually the first step to healing.

Chances are that there are many people in your life today in desperate need of healing. Perhaps you are even in need of healing yourself. Maybe your faith is gone and your hope is dead. Maybe you are battle-worn and desperately tired, like I am as I write this chapter. Maybe love has abandoned you and grace has eluded you.

It's times like this when we need to put simple love into action. When we are at the end of ourselves, we simply do not have the strength to move mountains with our love. In his book *Seeds of Greatness,* Denis Waitley gives the following acronym for love:

> L—listening when another is speaking
> O—overlooking petty faults and forgiving failures
> V—valuing other people for who they are
> E—expressing love in a practical way"[1]

When we are worn out and run down it does not give us an excuse to stop loving others. It just might be time to return to simpler tactics. Listen, overlook, value, and express. Those are four easy things to remember (although they may be harder to do) on a long and difficult day.

Love never fails, and the One who fills us with His love will not fail us in times when we have nothing left to give. He will give us a limitless supply if we simply call upon Him.

Sometimes He lets us get to a place where we are empty so that we *will* call upon Him.

TO LOVE AND BE LOVED

This chapter isn't so much on being a girl who loves as it is on being a girl *who is loved*. Sometimes we have to come to a place in our lives where we realize just how great love is. If you have spent even one day feeling like Patty, the beggar at the temple gate, or the thief on the cross—alone, abandoned, worthless, afraid—then you know how great it feels when someone stops and gives you five minutes of their time.

Each of us has wounds. Maybe your parents got divorced and you feel as if you have been put in the middle, or that you have been completely forgotten by one or both of your parents. Perhaps your parents are still married, but you have a ton of siblings, and you feel as if you are always compared to a brother or sister who seems to be your parents' favorite.

Maybe you are the only one of your friends who scored low on your SATs or didn't get asked to the school dance. Perhaps on the outside you look like you have it all— straight A's, a college scholarship, popularity, a nice car, and maybe even a cute boyfriend—but you feel like it has been quite some time since anyone has seen you for who you really are, and not just what you have.

At one point or another something will come into your life and hurt you. It happens to all of us. There will be a day when you have to overcome pain if you want to go on. Sometimes the fight will be long and hard. But that makes the victory greater. Today might be a day when faith and hope are waning, but they still exist. Love, however, is such a foreign concept that you wouldn't know what to do if it knocked on your door and invited itself inside.

You Are God's Beloved

For a while I wrestled with whether or not this chapter was necessary. But then they came, and continued to come, in abundance. One by one, girl by girl—some through e-mail, others in person—they came to me to tell me their stories. Each story was unique, but there were many underlying similarities. Each girl had her heart broken—some by parents, some by friends, some by a guy, and some by Christians they looked up to and respected.

These girls had lost faith; many were only hanging on to hope by a thread. With tearstained faces and aching hearts they were crying out for help. Slowly, patiently, and genuinely I gave all of these girls the same message.

I reminded them that they were the *beloved of God*. I pointed them to countless verses like Isaiah 49:15–16, which says:

> "Can a woman forget her nursing child, and have no compassion on the son of her womb? Even these may forget, but I will not forget you. Behold, I have inscribed you on the palms of My hands."

For some, God's love was not enough; they continued to

search for love in other places. But for many the change was slow yet radical. Coming to understand that you are the beloved of God changes your whole outlook on life. Love restores faith and hope. You can have faith without having hope and love, you can have hope without having faith and love, but having love always ensures that faith and hope will follow. No wonder the Bible says it's the greatest!

So now the question becomes, What do we do with love once we realize it has been given to us by God himself? Easier said than done, *we give it away*. We give of our time, talents, and resources to the people God has placed in our lives. It means that we share our lives with other people and we fill the lack of love in the lives of others with the abundance of love God has given us.

You can only give love freely when you understand how great it is. Until then you will keep blowing by people in fast food parking lots, like I almost blew by Patty. And you will keep on making rude comments—or at least listening to rude comments made by others—about the girl in school who is just a little different from everyone else.

Love is the greatest because it brings everything else with it. It may not always be able to fill a hungry tummy, but it can always warm a hurting heart. It may not bring back a lost loved one, but it can create a new one. It may not erase an ugly scar on someone's heart, but it can heal it. Without love, though, the rich are really poor, the smart are really ignorant, and the beautiful are really ugly.

Love changes lives, love saves lives, love makes lives what they really are. Of course love is the greatest! It is the most costly gift in the entire world, yet it is so easy to give away. Just a little bit goes a long way.

Why, then, do we hoard it? Why do we give it only begrudgingly and sparingly? Maybe it's because we fail to realize that God's love comes in an endless supply. We think that if we give it all away there will be nothing left for us. We're afraid we will run out—or perhaps we believe we already have.

Recently I saw a slogan on a jewelry store flyer that said, "True love stories never have an ending." That's certainly true of God's love for each and every one of us—it goes on and on and on. His love supply never runs dry, so we can keep on loving others

> *God's love comes in an endless supply.*

minute by minute, hour by hour, day by day for the rest of our lives. It means that we have enough love to give some away to people like Patty in parking lots or homeless shelters. And we will still have enough left over to bring home at the end of the day to the friends and family that we love most.

Imagine that—one simple thing can last forever, come in endless supply, heal the brokenhearted, warm a cold and lonely soul, be given away over and over again to anyone and everyone you meet ... and in the end you will always have more than enough left over.

Does that sound too good to be true? It's not. Try it for yourself and see. I promise: It's the greatest.

FOR FURTHER THOUGHT:

1. Who do you blow by on a regular basis that is desperately in need of love?

2. What are some things you can do to show love to him/her/them?

3. Do you regularly view yourself as the beloved of God?

4. What are some key verses you can use to remind yourself that you are God's beloved?

5. What are some simple ways you can "give love away" to those around you?

LOVE IN ACTION:

Make a conscious effort to see the people you normally pass without noticing. Take some extra time and start up a conversation, or buy them a warm meal. Maybe there is a girl who sits alone at lunch or break at school. Try talking to her or inviting her to sit with you. Perhaps you have a grumpy old neighbor who never says hello to anyone. Try making an effort to be friendly the next time you see him or her. Maybe you have a teacher who is gruff and a mean old grouch. Bring him or her a little treat and let him or her know you enjoy the class. In college my husband simply said "thank you" to a professor who was handing out tests, and the man stopped and practically broke down because that was the first time a student said that to him. This later opened the door for my husband to share his faith with his professor. Kindness and courtesy are characteristics of love—and people will notice them. A little love really does go a long way. Step out of your comfort zone and give love to someone who desperately needs it. Show them you know love is the greatest.

Notes

1. As quoted in Charles R. Swindoll's *The Tale of the Tardy Ox Cart* (Nashville: Word Publishing, 1998), 359.

3

Loving the Unlovable

We all have them in our lives. You know exactly the type of people I am talking about. They are rude, selfish, malicious—and they just rub you the wrong way. The best way to describe them is unlovable. The biggest problem with unlovable people is that we *are* called to love them, and not only that, but we are called to love them *as they are.*

Notice the Bible doesn't tell us to wait until they become lovable—because they may never do that. In Luke 6:27–29 Jesus says:

> "But I say to you who hear, love your enemies, do good to those who hate you, bless those who curse you, pray for those who mistreat you.
>
> "Whoever hits you on the cheek, offer him the other also; and whoever takes away your coat, do not withhold your shirt from him either."

In verse 35 of that same chapter He adds:

> "But love your enemies, and do good, and lend, expecting nothing in return; and your reward will be great, and you

will be sons of the Most High; and He Himself is kind to ungrateful and evil men."

Yes, you have unlovable people in your life. We all do. That's not your problem. Your problem is probably the same problem I have—you don't really *want* to learn how to love them.

Unlovable people are usually not in short supply.

You would rather just leave them alone—or make them pay. I'm sure that if I asked you to think of three people whom you would deem mean and just plain unlovable, you could most likely give me a list of ten. Unlovable people are usually not in short supply. My friend Kathy calls them "sandpaper people." When I think of things I want to do in my life, being sanded down by other people is not one of them.

LESSONS FIT FOR A KING

When I think of this process, King David always comes to mind. He was sanded down by the king who preceded him, Saul, until there was almost nothing left. Both were the Lord's anointed. Over time, though, Saul felt threatened by David and feared he would lose his kingdom. This drove him absolutely mad—and we all know there is nothing worse than a crazy person with power.

Let's take a look at the history behind their story. Saul was anointed king; he disobeyed God on more than one occasion, so God sent His prophet Samuel to choose another king to replace him. Thus David was anointed while still just a teen.

But instead of passing *Go*, collecting $200, and moving straight to the throne, David was sent back to the pasture to tend his sheep. When war broke out he was quickly promoted to pizza delivery man so he could take food out to his brothers who were in battle against the Philistines.

As we all know, there on the battlefield David the shepherd boy became David the warrior. He killed a giant with a leather sling and one smooth stone. David then moved from warrior to musician, as King Saul's harp player, and was welcomed into the palace that he would someday take over.

The people loved David—the king even loved David—yet Saul was afraid of David because he was a threat to his kingdom. And that's where we'll pick up the story. First Samuel 18:5–9 says:

> So David went out wherever Saul sent him, and prospered; and Saul set him over the men of war. And it was pleasing in the sight of all the people and also in the sight of Saul's servants.
>
> And it happened as they were coming, when David returned from killing the Philistine, that the women came out of all the cities of Israel, singing and dancing, to meet King Saul, with tambourines, with joy and with musical instruments.

And the women sang as they played, and said, "Saul has slain his thousands, and David his ten thousands." Then Saul became very angry, for this saying displeased him; and he said, "They have ascribed to David ten thousands, but to me they have ascribed thousands. Now what more can he have but the kingdom?"

And Saul looked at David with suspicion from that day on.

It was Saul's jealousy and insecurity that made him the ruthless and mean man he became. He felt threatened by David. Perhaps the unlovable people in your life somehow feel threatened by you as well. When we begin to see the unlovable people in our lives as the insecure individuals they are, it makes it harder to be angry with them—and easier to love them. Look at how Saul's jealousy drove him to ruin in verses 10–16:

Now it came about on the next day that an evil spirit from God came mightily upon Saul, and he raved in the midst of the house, while David was playing the harp with his hand, as usual; and a spear was in Saul's hand.

And Saul hurled the spear for he thought, "I will pin David to the wall." But David escaped from his presence twice. Now Saul was afraid of David, for the Lord was with him but had departed from Saul.

Therefore Saul removed him from his presence, and appointed him as his commander of a thousand; and he went out and came in before the people.

And David was prospering in all his ways for the Lord was with him. When Saul saw that he was prospering greatly, he dreaded him. But all Israel and Judah loved David, and he went out and came in before them.

Jumping down to verses 28–29 we read:

When Saul saw and knew that the Lord was with David, and that Michal, Saul's daughter, loved him, then Saul was even more afraid of David. Thus Saul was David's enemy continually.

Sadly, the story does not end there. Saul winds up driving David out of the kingdom, sending him running for his life. Wrongly accused, David shakes hands with death several times as he is hiding out in caves, fiercely sought after by Saul and his men. Saul was the epitome of an unlovable person.

The Same Problems Face Us Too

Do you have someone in your life seeking to devour you the way Saul attempted to devour David? Are you running for your life, hiding in your own caves, and begging God to save you?

Is someone out there slandering your reputation, trying to rile you up and make you mad just so you look bad in front of others? Is there someone in your life who looks at you as a threat? Maybe they've even gone the next step—they've declared war on you because they see you as an enemy.

Recently I received a phone call and a frantic e-mail from a friend who just went off to college. Not even a month into her semester, she was already having roommate conflicts. In tears she wailed, "My roommate is spreading rumors around campus that I am a big flirt and that I am with many different guys at one time." She was probably especially surprised to be facing this at a Christian college.

"Why would she do that? Why would she try to ruin my reputation like that?" My friend was naïve and didn't recognize the traces of King Saul in her roommate.

"Are you getting attention from guys?" My question was supposed to be helpful, although I'm not sure if it was initially received that way or not.

"Well, yeah," my friend responded, pausing because she was not sure where I was going.

"Do you think your roommate might want some of that attention?" By this point I was hoping my friend would catch on to what was really happening behind the scenes.

"Yeah," she said after a longer pause. "She really *is* a big flirt," she added.

"Maybe, just maybe," I said, "she is trying to level the playing field and take you out of the game."

"Why would she want to cause conflict?" My friend's question was sincere.

"Because she is jealous," I said. "Roommate or no roommate, you are viewed as competition, and she's doing all she can to defeat you."

LEARNING TO LOVE THOSE WE JUST CAN'T

Girls can be mean. Very mean. Especially when it comes to guys or spots on a sports team or a moment in the spotlight. In high school, four girls who were supposedly my friends had my name removed from the homecoming ballot the day before voting took place because I wouldn't party with them over the weekend. They wanted to teach me that popularity has a price, and they tried to punish me because I wasn't willing to pay it.

If David's life teaches us anything about loving the unlovable it is this: Love them from a distance and leave them in God's hands. In the end He will keep them from prevailing against us. We do have to keep in mind, however, that our idea of prevailing and God's idea of prevailing may be two entirely different things.

In 1 Samuel 23:14 it says regarding David, "And Saul sought him every day, but God did not deliver him into his hand." The good news is that although the battle rages, although you may get hurt, your popularity may wane, and the enemy may be clawing at your back door, God will not deliver you into the hands of those who seek to destroy you.

Proverbs 10:24–25 says, "What the wicked fears will come upon him, and the desire of the righteous will be granted. When the whirlwind passes, the wicked is no more, but the righteous has an everlasting foundation."

God will only let the wicked—and unlovable—get so far before pulling you from their grasp. *Why?* you might ask. *Why would He even let them touch me at all? Why doesn't God stop them before I have to suffer?*

Those aren't fun questions, and they don't have a fun answer. Simply put, it's because God wants to teach you to love the unlovable.

In *A Tale of Three Kings*, Gene Edwards says this about those of us who are spending all of our time focusing on the one—or ones—who are so aggressively pursuing us:

> You have your eyes on the wrong King Saul. As long as you look at your king, you will blame him and him alone, for your present hell. Be careful, for God has *His* eyes fastened sharply on *another* King Saul. One just as bad—or worse. God is looking at the King Saul in *you*.[1]

Edwards goes on to talk about how the tool God used to prevent the inner Saul in David from ruining him was the outer Saul that sat on Israel's throne. He claims that the years Saul sought to destroy David were years where David's heart was mutilated and his personality was altered forever. But it worked. David never became like Saul.

Do you respond to your own sacred surgery with the grace that David showed? Or do you put up a fight? Do you pick up spears and throw them back? Do you come out of the caves demanding your own rights and starting an all-out war?

LETTING YOUR CHARACTER SHINE

What did David do that was so noble? How did he love the unlovable King Saul?

First Samuel 24:1–7 says:

BEING A GIRL WHO LOVES

Now it came about when Saul returned from pursuing the Philistines, he was told, saying, "Behold, David is in the wilderness of Engedi."

Then Saul took three thousand chosen men from all Israel, and went to seek David and his men in front of the Rocks of the Wild Goats.

And he came to the sheepfolds on the way, where there was a cave; and Saul went in to relieve himself. Now David and his men were sitting in the inner recesses of the cave.

And the men of David said to him, "Behold this is the day of which the Lord said to you, 'Behold; I am about to give your enemy into your hand, and you shall do to him as it seems good to you.'" Then David arose and cut off the edge of Saul's robe secretly.

And it came about afterward that David's conscience bothered him because he had cut off the edge of Saul's robe.

So he said to his men, "Far be it from me because of the Lord that I should do this thing to my lord, the Lord's anointed, to stretch out my hand against him, since he is the Lord's anointed."

And David persuaded his men with these words and did not allow them to rise up against Saul. And Saul arose, left the cave, and went on his way.

Hmmm. It looks like David mastered Jesus' command in Luke 6:27 although it had not even been uttered yet. When was the last time you loved your enemies and did good to those who persecuted *you?*

When was the last time you did what Luke 6:28 says and

prayed for those who mistreat you? And I don't mean praying that God would pour wrath on them—I mean praying that God would heal their hurts and bring them joy, thus changing them in the process. When was the last time you chose not to fight back and retaliate even though everyone around you was telling you that fighting back was the right thing to do?

David did that not once, but twice. First Samuel 26 tells the story of how David once entered Saul's camp while Saul and his men were sleeping. What an opportunity! But David simply took a water jug and a spear, and left, sparing their lives.

He could have ended his own agony in a brief moment. He could have taken Saul's life and made himself king. Yet he spared his enemy and let him live. When Saul went for David's right cheek, David turned and gave him his left. And you know what happened?

Five chapters later Saul died by his own sword. He was wounded in battle and took his own life. When the Philistines found him, they chopped off his head and fastened his body to the city wall, mocking his defeat. What was David's response to this turn of events?

Second Samuel 1:11–12 tells us that he tore his clothes and mourned, weeping and fasting all day long. He didn't throw a party when he inherited his throne. He was not self-seeking. He was not boastful. It sounds like he had the characteristics of 1 Corinthians 13 down pretty well—and they weren't even written yet. And he didn't just demonstrate this kind of love with Saul. Years later, when David's own son Absalom tried to overthrow David's kingdom and make himself king, David exercised that same grace and love and did not seek to destroy Absalom. In fact, David even told his men not to harm him, and when word of Absolom's death reached David, he wept and mourned for him much the same way he did for Saul (2 Samuel 18). That's just amazing to me.

No wonder God called David a man after His own heart! Despite his flaws and failures, David's *character* was truly admirable.

Let's look at 1 Corinthians 13:4–8 again:

> Love is patient, love is kind, and is not jealous; love does not brag and is not arrogant, does not act unbecomingly; it does not seek its own, is not provoked, does not take into account a wrong suffered, does not rejoice in unrighteousness, but rejoices with the truth; bears all things, believes all things, hopes all things, endures all things. Love never fails.

Never? Not even when the person you are trying to love is unlovable? *Nope, not even then.* David lived a whole decade between his anointing and his inauguration. For ten long years his life was made pure hell by a mad king. There was no definite end in sight, no predetermined date that would liberate him from his agony.

Yet David loved anyway, and his actions leave us without excuse—we must seek to do the same. If David could love a spear-chucking king who sought his life on many occasions, we can definitely love those who are doing far less harm to us.

Sometimes there is no obvious end in sight to our agony either. Many times it takes a while for the day of our liberation to arrive. But we are to love those difficult people in the meantime. And *how* do we love them? The same way that we love those who are very lovable.

We love them with everything we've got. We let the unlovable people in our lives be themselves. We don't try to change them, we don't try to control them, and we don't try to dominate them.

> ## We let God have His way with them.

Instead, we let God have His way with them. They will eventually make a turn around or—like Saul—die on their own sword. When God brings unlovable people into our lives we need to realize something:

Those who are hurt, hurt others. Somewhere along the line these people have been rejected. They went looking for love and did not find it. As a result, insecurity rules them and fear reigns in their very souls. Sometimes people like this will soften over time if we persistently love them. Persistence is hard when they are grinding at our every nerve. But 1 Corinthians 13 says love is *patient* for a reason.

LIVING WITH THE UNLOVABLE

In college I had one of the most unloving roommates of all time. We'll call her Tiffany. One night she and I were the only ones home—our other roommate was out with her boyfriend for the evening.

I was very sick that night. I had a really bad sinus infection, and the only thing that was keeping me out of bed was the fact that I had a paper due the next morning. I had the chills, my nose was running, and I felt like I couldn't breathe. It was raining outside, and I was just miserable. Then Tiffany decided to do the most amazing thing: She turned on the air-conditioning.

"Tiffany," I finally asked when my bedroom began to feel like I was out in a blizzard, "It's pretty cool in here now. Do you think we can turn the air off?"

"No," she said flatly without turning away from her computer screen. By this point my teeth were chattering.

"I'm really sick," I finally said, "and I would appreciate it if we could turn the air off."

With fire in her eyes she turned to me and said, "You are cold. I am hot. You can easily put a jacket on to warm up; there is nothing I can do to cool down."

Shivering the whole way, I went to my closet and put on my large pea coat, a beanie, and some gloves. I think I may have even found a scarf. For half an hour I sat at my computer, trying to work my frozen fingers over the keys on my keyboard while wiping my nose until it was raw. Finally I got up to turn the air off myself, and Tiffany freaked out.

"What do you think you are doing?" She lit into me with fury and proceeded to call *me* selfish when *I* was the one running a fever, bundled up like an Eskimo, and now less than twenty-four hours away from turning in a paper that I could not write under these ridiculous circumstances.

Finally she grabbed her stuff, slammed the door, and left in a mad huff. She was one of the hardest people I ever had to learn to love. But with God's grace it got easier throughout the school year.

Another time when I was in college and still living in the dorms, I had to share *two* washing machines and *two* dryers with *sixty* other girls. Doing laundry in the dorms was never fun. No matter what hour of day you went into our little laundry room, the washer and dryer were both working overtime, and there was a line of laundry baskets piled high with a week's worth of items waiting for their turn to be made clean.

Upperclassmen knew from years of experience that in order to have clean clothes every week you had to come up with a laundry-washing *strategy*. You could not, under any circumstances, think that you were going to simply walk into the laundry room and wash your clothes and then walk back out without having to wait for, fight over, or share the machines. Things just didn't work that way in Alpha Chi.

Since I was raised as an only child, going away to a living situation like that was a major growth experience for me. Imagine how I felt one night when I walked into the laundry room to find my wet clothes had been removed from the washer and tossed onto the very dirty tile floor. I was furious.

It was all I could do not to pack my bags and go home right then! What I really wanted to do was hunt down the culprit and demand an answer for why she had done this. Instead, I simply wrote a note in the floor folder on our Internet bulletin board, letting whoever she was know that I was not happy with her. I also told her she needed to make sure she never did that again.

Then I gathered up my now filthy clothes, dumped them in my laundry basket, and prepared myself to once again wait for my turn to do laundry. I mean, where did this person grow up? Who in the world could have that little regard for some- one else's things? After that experience, doing laundry was even more of a chore than before. I became extra paranoid, imagining that if I left my clothes unattended in the laundry room for even five minutes they would be ruined forever.

Imagine my surprise a few weeks after that disheartening incident when I walked into the laundry room and found my freshly dried clothes had been removed from the dryer, folded, and placed neatly in my laundry basket. If there had been a mint sitting on top of them I would have sworn I was in a hotel. I was so touched by that simple act of kindness that I casually asked around the floor for weeks, trying to find out who did it.

When no one admitted doing it, I wrote a happy and colorful little note and hung it on the laundry room door, thanking my mystery person for blessing me in such a nice way. How many people do you know that willingly fold someone else's underwear?

A few weeks later, I repaid the favor and folded someone

else's clothes. For the rest of the semester our laundry room door was plastered with thank-you notes because that one simple act of kindness had become contagious and was now being reciprocated by many girls.

Even a simple (or torturous, depending on how you look at it) task like doing laundry can be done in love. When it was, it changed the whole atmosphere of our dorm floor and lifted everyone's spirits. One unloving person's cruel and self-ish act can be reversed by another person's kind and loving act.

Singing or Screaming

Even when someone does something unlovable to you, you can choose to do something loving in return. You have two choices when you are being tried by the unlovable people in your life. You can either scream or you can sing. Which would you rather hear? I don't know about you, but the sound of screaming is not pleasing to my ears. And I'm sure God doesn't really enjoy it much either.

Singing, however, is quite a different story. In the laundry room situation I started with screaming and ended with singing, which produced a much better result.

King David was a singer. Just read through the Psalms. He was quite a composer for a caveman! Song after song was written in the dark caves and other hideouts David inhabited while Saul was seeking his life. After fleeing Saul on one occasion, David penned the words of Psalm 57. Verse seven says this: "My heart is steadfast, O God, my heart is steadfast; I will sing, yes, I will sing praises!"

What about you? Do you sing? Or do you scream? God can do a lot with the one, but there's not much He can do with the other.

When it comes to loving the unlovable, the rules are still the same. Love is not about the one loving but about the one being loved.

First Corinthians 13 is still the standard. And King David is a good example.

I remember being in junior high, and in my particular group of girl friends, someone was always being pushed out. She was the "attack victim of the week"—which meant she was ostracized and not spoken to by the others. When her week-long penalty was over for whatever reason, she was welcomed back into the circle.

I found myself shut out many times. But on one particular day my friend April was the one taking the beating. She came to me pleading, thinking I would understand her pain.

But at this particular time in my life, I was too immature to care about anyone's pain but my own. And as long as she was on the outside, I was on the inside—and that made me happy. So I fueled the fire. I heaped on the insults. And the emotional stress placed on April during day one of her week-long ousting was so great that she left school early.

I ran into her on her way to the office to leave and I remember telling her something like, "I have no pity on you because I have endured weeks of what you are going through. You're a wimp if you can't even handle a day. You deserve whatever comes to you."

That was over ten years ago, and I wince every time I think of that day. For one brief moment I thought it was okay to be unloving if you felt unloved yourself. And I did some major damage in the life of this particular girl. I looked in the mirror expecting to see David, and instead I found Saul.

Who do you see when you look in the mirror? Often, the most unlovable person in our life is a mirror of our greatest flaws.

God brings people like that into our lives so that we can be sanded down and over time made into His own image. Just like God used the outer Saul to kill the inner Saul in David, He uses the unlovable traits in others to kill those very same traits in us.

Think for a moment about the most unlovable person in your life. What is it that you like least about them? Be honest. How much of that same trait do you see in yourself?

Are you letting God use your sandpaper people to sand you down and make you more like Him? Or are you letting other people drive you mad, like King Saul did?

You better be careful, because if you start going mad like King Saul, you too might die by your own sword.

FOR FURTHER THOUGHT:

1. Think of someone who is hard for you to love. How have they treated you? How have you treated them in return?

2. What can you personally learn from the story of Saul and David?

3. Are you more prone to sing or scream? Why?

4. Name a time when you were an unlovable person. What caused you to be this way?

5. When you examine the unlovable person (or people) in your life, can you see where he/she/they might be jealous or insecure? How does this affect his/her/their behavior?

LOVE IN ACTION:

Find one unlovable person, then look for an area she seems to be insecure about and build her up in that area. For example, if there is a girl at school who is unattractive but she always makes fun of the way you dress and do your hair, find something about her appearance that you can compliment. Be honest. If you like her hair, tell her. If her new shoes are cute, say so. And be sincere in how you do it. If you keep it up, it just might change the way she treats you. If it doesn't, you still haven't lost anything by being nice. Remember, *love isn't about the one doing the loving, but about the one being loved.* Building an insecure person's confidence will definitely do him or her good in the long run, and it won't really cost you a thing.

Notes

1. Gene Edwards, *A Tale of Three Kings* (Wheaton, IL: Tyndale House Publishers, 1992), 21.

4

All in the Family

He was set to be king. Royalty was his birthright. From childhood he had been groomed to take over the kingdom. So why would he give it all up? As a strong warrior, Jonathan was the perfect successor in Saul's eyes. But God had His eyes on another person to become king, and Jonathan was wise enough to recognize that. So he stripped himself of his royal garments and preserved David's life when Saul viciously tried to take it time after time. Jonathan helped David to the kingdom—*Jonathan's* kingdom. Why? Because 1 Samuel 18:1 tells us, "Jonathan loved him [David] as himself."

The previous chapter used David and Saul's story to demonstrate what loving the unlovable looks like. This chapter focuses on the brotherly love Jonathan—Saul's son—demonstrated to David during that same time.

In a cutthroat world where people are always attempting to take what is "rightfully theirs," Christians can easily fall into the trap of fighting for their own rights and privileges while mindlessly trampling on others or meeting their own needs at the expense of someone else. Girls especially fall victim to this mentality, often fighting over silly stuff like boys and popularity. Sometimes Christian girls will even fight over who is more spiritual or the most gifted! And in the gray areas of dating and courting, it's common for Christians to fight over what is the most godly way to behave.

At times like these we forget something very important: We are all part of the family of Christ. Tragically, we find ourselves bickering, manipulating, and sometimes even downright attacking our brothers and sisters in the Lord even as we gather at the Lord's Table. Paul had strong words for the Corinthian believers who were engaging in this kind of unloving behavior (1 Corinthians 11:17–34). We usually do this for one of two reasons—we are either jealous or insecure. Sometimes we are both.

In high school I had a crush on a certain boy in our youth group. One night one of the girls on the leadership team with me called to ask if I had feelings for this boy. When I said yes, she answered, "Well, I do too, and I didn't want this to be a *silent* competition." With that she hung up the phone and altered our friendship forever.

I used to think petty bickering was something that eventually disappeared with age. Recently, though, I have spoken at several women's retreats and found that the forty- and fifty-year-old women respond to messages on friendship much the same way that teenage girls do. They come forward with broken hearts because of the way they have been treated and repentant spirits for the way they have treated others.

SURRENDERING THE UPPER HAND

Pettiness may not disappear with age, but it does disappear with *maturity*. When you get to a place where you can recognize and acknowledge your own jealousy and insecurities, you can actually grow through the experience and get past your pettiness. Then it becomes much easier to love everyone in the family of Christ.

As proof that age is not the factor that determines maturity, Jonathan and David were mere teenagers when their story began. One of them was *born* to be king; the other was *destined* to be king. Although Jonathan held the keys to the kingdom in his hands, he was wise enough to know when God had spoken, and he willingly placed his crown on David's head. Yes, David was a man after God's own heart. But many commentators point to Jonathan as the one who exemplified Jesus' command to lay down one's life for his friends.

As we know, Saul, Jonathan's father, was the king of Israel. In the beginning he seemed to be a good ruler, until his heart grew hard. The contrast between this father and son is amazing. Jonathan willingly surrendered the crown he would one day inherit, while Saul clung tightly to the crown that was quickly passing from his hands. After David killed Goliath, promoting himself from shepherd boy to war hero, and capturing the attention of the king, a beautiful friendship formed between him and Jonathan.

First Samuel 18:1–4 says:

> Now it came about when he had finished speaking to

Saul, that the soul of Jonathan was knit to the soul of David, and Jonathan loved him as himself.

And Saul took him that day and did not let him return to his father's house.

Then Jonathan made a covenant with David because he loved him as himself.

And Jonathan stripped himself of the robe that was on him and gave it to David, with his armor, including his sword and his bow and his belt.

The sword, the bow, and the belt were very symbolic gifts to give to someone else. Many commentators agree that in this passage, Jonathan was symbolically transferring his kingdom into David's hands. Imagine that! Here is a guy groomed to be king, who spots another young, good-looking candidate for the task. Jonathan knew there were only two ways David could ever obtain his kingdom. Jonathan would have to surrender it, or David would have to take it by force—and David wasn't exactly the taking type.

So Jonathan, who did not give in to the petty jealousy that we see so often among Christians today, came alongside of David and gave him not only his kingdom but also the love and encouragement he would need to become an excellent king. In 1 Samuel 19, when Saul seeks to put David to death, Jonathan warns David and then goes before Saul on David's behalf to encourage Saul to let David live.

Hello! That was Jonathan's sure shot to obtaining the kingdom he *rightfully* deserved. He could have easily looked the other way as Saul had David killed, ending any potential threat to Jonathan's throne. Jonathan would not have even had any blood on his own hands. But Jonathan's love for David was greater than any desire for the kingdom. It was greater than any position, any popularity, or any wealth.

And Jonathan does not do this only once. He continues to defend David before Saul, until Saul finally grows angry with him and says in 1 Samuel 20:31, "For as long as the son of Jesse lives on the earth, neither you nor your kingdom will be established." Jonathan knew that was true. But he still defends David to his father and goes out into the field to warn David to run for his life. As the two weep together, Jonathan says to David, "Go in safety, inasmuch as we have sworn to each other in the name of the Lord, saying, 'The Lord will be between me and you, and between my descendants and your descendents forever'" (1 Samuel 20:42).

Later, when David hears of Jonathan's death in battle, he tears his clothes and weeps, saying, "I am distressed for you, my brother Jonathan; you have been very pleasant to me. Your love to me was more wonderful than the love of women" (2 Samuel 1:26). That right there is brotherly love as its finest. Once David was finally settled into his kingdom—the kingdom he knew Jonathan gave up for him—he asked if there was anyone left of Saul's household that he could show kindness to for Jonathan's sake. His servants told him of Jonathan's son, Mephibosheth, who was crippled in both feet and hiding out in a distant village for fear of being killed.

Moved with compassion for his friend who gave him everything, David sent for Mephibosheth and invited him to eat at his royal table. He provided him with servants and treated him as one of his own sons. Technically, the custom of that time period was to put to death any relatives remaining from the previous ruler so that they would not pose a threat to the new kingdom. But David, remembering that Jonathan spared his life and essentially made him king, spared Mephibosheth's life and restored him to the position of prince.

That's what Romans 12:10 means when it says, "Be devoted to one another in brotherly love; give preference to one another in honor." Jonathan and David's story is a story of the surrendering of rights, of the laying down of lives, of loving with all you have until the very end. They exemplify what Christian love should look like. Anything less is unacceptable for people in God's family.

SAME FAMILY, DIFFERENT APPROACHES TO LIFE

So what about you? Are you a Saul or a Jonathan? The difference between the two men is simply this: Saul was driven by fear and insecurity, and Jonathan was driven by love. The temptation to be like Saul is always there in each of us. A new girl threatens our popularity at school, so we choose not to like her. Our friend gets her hair cut in a really cute style but we pretend not to like it, so she doesn't know how cute it really is. A friend gets asked to the school dance by the guy of our dreams, and we try to guilt her out of going with him—even though we would have gone if he had asked us. The list could go on and on.

Each time something like this happens, the enemy's voice always whispers the same thing: *Drive her out of your kingdom. Do not let her sit on your throne. Annihilate her.* And many times we do. Most of the time, being like Jonathan doesn't even cross our minds. To many of us, his story is probably only vaguely familiar. It's just so much easier to be like Saul!

But over and over again the Lord commands us to love one another, not to shove one another. The Christian life is one of continual surrender. Many times it means surrendering our rights—or even the upper hand—to those who are undeserving. Sometimes the most undeserving people of all are those who are also part of God's family. In my short life I have met some very hurtful and hateful Christians. But their behavior does not give me an excuse to be hurtful or hateful in return.

> *The Christian life is one of continual surrender.*

The brotherly love Romans 12:10 talks about gives *preference* to one another. That means it gives its best—even when other people are not giving theirs. It means accepting people as they are and not trying to change them. It means allowing people to do things their way and not how you think they should be done. It means giving them grace even when they don't deserve it. Love means giving people your seat at the table when there isn't one reserved for them.

Fighting for a Place in the Family

Too often Christians fight with other Christians about *Christian things*. Someone thinks she would be a better worship leader than someone else, so she attacks the person in the position ruthlessly. Often girls are gossip queens—which is not a good thing. And many times we use the cover of "prayer requests" to spread other people's personal business around the youth group. You know how it goes. Sometimes the truth is even stretched.

"My friend Katie is dating a non-Christian guy; I think she might even be sleeping with him. So pray for her, okay?" Yes, it is good to pray for your friends, but the Bible does not tell us to go and shout other people's sin (or suspected sin) from the rooftops. So why is it that we feel we can openly talk about other people's sin as long as we are praying for them?

The Bible does not say, "Don't gossip, unless you pray and gossip at the same time." It simply says not to gossip. Proverbs 20:19 tells us not to even associate with gossips, much less be one. And in 2 Corinthians 12:20 Paul lists gossip in a group of sins that he fears has taken over the church. Many times when we talk about other people, especially other Christians, we are doing it to make ourselves feel better. We have little or no regard for the feelings of the person we are discussing.

It seems to me that, in the family of Christ, we are always looking for reasons to nitpick and tear others down. We are far too quick to point the finger. When I was in high school, one of our youth *leaders* stopped my mom in the supermarket to inform her that I had missed youth group for two weeks in a row. She went on to say that she knew I must have backslidden and fallen into sin, and she just wanted to let my mom know. Imagine how this youth leader must have felt when my mom informed her that I was in the hospital for major surgery!

I attended a retreat recently where a workshop was being offered entitled "Choose not to be offended." When the speaker got up to share about her topic, she said she really should have titled it "Choose not to be *offensive*." That really stuck with me. So many times we self-righteously hold our heads up high and treat other Christians as if they are dirt under our feet.

They're Not Perfect, but Neither Are You

We have come to understand the concept of grace in regard to what it means for us: We are forgiven and loved by God no matter what we have done. Yet we are prone to hold grudges when it comes to others who have wronged us, which is of course the very opposite of grace. All too often I have seen youth groups divided over petty and stupid things. And many times youth pastors and youth leaders are right up there in the forefront of the conflict, fueling the fire and modeling destructive habits.

As a youth leader, I am sorry that our examples are not always perfect. I am sorry that at times you have even been taught to be a grace killer or a finger pointer by those you trusted to teach you and lead you. None of us is perfect, yet we are all without excuse. First John 3:10 clearly tells us that if we do not love our brothers and sisters in the Lord, we are not of God.

That doesn't leave us much room to grow bitter, hold grudges, or spread gossip. But bad habits are hard to break—especially when we are surrounded by others who practice them. So how do we as individuals tune out what others are doing and focus on loving others the way the Bible tells us to, whether they love us in return or not?

We do this by applying ourselves to loving other people. We use love as a verb and put it into action. Someone once told me the secret to truly loving other Christians was found in the acronym JOY. It helped to put priorities in order: Jesus, Others, then Yourself. Putting others before yourself is not a natural response. It takes an active effort.

It means thinking through each and every situation. Before you join in the conversation about how so-and-so has begun to dress really immodestly lately, you need to think about how so-and-so would feel if she knew people were talking behind her back. Before you share a friend's prayer request, you might want to consider why she didn't share it herself. Before you attempt to critique the way someone else is serving the Lord in ministry, you need to remember that God called *her* to do it for now and not *you*.

And when you feel as if another Christian is trying your patience beyond belief, you need to remember Jonathan—the prince that surrendered his kingdom. He did not demand his own rights, he did not fight for his own crown, but instead he was a picture of Jesus himself when he laid everything down for the sake of someone who was unworthy.

The people in your life are probably unworthy of love and grace at times too. But that does not mean that we should withhold love and grace from them. Proverbs 17:17 says, "A friend loves at all times." That means a true friend loves even when she is not being loved back.

Love is always a choice. Who is more important, the other person or you? Jesus gave us an example to follow, but we fail miserably most of the time. Life is hard, and love is even harder. If it was easy, the world would be a far different place.

I had a roommate in college who had a very annoying habit. Every time one of us said something like, "I can't believe I have to take the trash out in the rain," my roommate would reply, "You don't have to. *You get to.*" Many times we look at life in terms of, "I *have* to love so-and-so because God says I have to." Imagine how differently we would behave if our perspective was, "I *get* to love so-and-so because the Bible tells me to, and God promises to give me the strength to love them." People are the only relational creatures God made. Sure, animals mate and cohabit, but they do not live, laugh, and love like humans do.

> *People are the only relational creatures God made.*

It is a privilege to love and be loved. Yet many times we do not live like we believe that. Instead, we live like it is a torturous task or a prison sentence. But love is a gift. It is always a gift, whether we give it or receive it. And gifts are always received in light of the attitude of the one giving it.

When my husband proposed to me, he gave me a beautiful engagement ring. He didn't give it to me because he had to—that would have ruined the whole experience. He gave it to me because he wanted to, and every day when I wear it my heart is filled with joy because it is a symbol of his great love for me.

When you give your words, your attitudes, and your actions to other people, do they feel as if you are giving them because you have to, or because you really want to? When you give love, do you really give it, or do you do it begrudgingly? Trust me, people know the difference.

Once when I was in junior high, I was out Christmas shopping with both of my parents. The stores were absolute bedlam. People were fighting over the last piece of everything, and I just wanted to go home. As we were heading through the parking lot we heard a frazzled mom yelling at the handful of children in her minivan while her husband stared off into space with a glazed look on his face.

"Now we are going to sit here until we are one nice, happy family," this woman screamed at the top of her lungs, her face turning purple. My parents and I looked at each other wide-eyed. When we got to our car we burst out laughing at the irony of that woman's statement and her method of communicating it. None of us has forgotten her since.

What about you? Do your actions toward other Christians scream something different than your words? Or are you pretty consistent? Does your philosophy of love match up to the one outlined in the Bible?

In life we always have two choices—we can make every effort to get along like a nice, happy family. Or we can leave the rest of the world shaking their heads as we scream at each other with purple faces in crowded parking lots. Which are you going to choose?

FOR FURTHER THOUGHT:

1. Which do you find it harder to love: other Christians or non-Christians? Why do you think that is?

2. List some things Christians fight about. Do you think that fighting is really necessary? Why or why not? What are some better ways to resolve disputes and settle differences?

3. List some ways our differences can work for the benefit of the kingdom of God.

4. Are you more like Saul or Jonathan? How so?

5. What are some ways you can make an active effort to bring unity to the body of Christ?

LOVE IN ACTION:

Find a Christian you tend to go to blows with, attempt to make peace with him or her, and surrender the upper hand to him or her in an area where the two of you tend to strive and struggle. Resist the urge to take it back and see what God does in the situation. (For example: If you are one of several girls singing on the youth group worship team, and there is usually competition and bickering over who gets to sing the solo, give it up without a fight next time.) If you honestly do this, God will either move in the situation to make things right, or He will move you to another place of service. Remember, Jonathan surrendered his crown, and God made the *right man* king. Things might not turn out how you want them to, but at least you will know you did your best to keep the peace in God's family.

5

Every Hour of Every Day

One night during small group time at the girls' Bible study I used to teach at my church, I shared a story about the sister of a girl I met the previous weekend at a women's retreat. Her name was Danielle, and when she was seventeen she was killed in a car accident on her way home from Bible study one evening. After her death, her parents found a list of names in her wallet of unsaved kids she wanted to see come to Christ. Many of the names were crossed off because she had already led them to the Lord. Four more were crossed off after her funeral.

Danielle was someone with incredible impact. She was a world changer. I challenged the girls in my group with Danielle's story, asking them if they loved others with the same fervor. After Bible study I got in my car for the long one-hour drive home with that story fresh in my mind. But it never once dawned on me that I might not make it home from Bible study that night.

The gas gauge in my car had been acting funny for a few weeks. Even right after I filled up, the needle would bounce around and land on empty. I'd been meaning to get it fixed, but the busyness of my life kept me from taking the time to have it checked out.

My drive home from Bible study was a dark one, through a deserted stretch of freeway with many hills and not much light. So I called my mom to check on the playoff baseball scores and to see how her day was. Chatting as I drove made the drive pass quickly and kept me awake on the dark roads.

When I was about twenty minutes into my drive, I noticed the warning light come up on my dashboard. When I had left the church my gauge had indicated that I had a quarter of a tank of gas—more than enough to get home. The needle, though, began to plunge rapidly. I wouldn't be near a gas station for miles, so I said a prayer and just kept going.

When I was about fifteen minutes farther, the needle was fluctuating between empty and very empty. But it had done that many times before, when it wasn't really empty, so I wasn't too concerned. When I was about ten minutes away from my house—and still on the freeway—I began to feel my car let up. If you have ever run out of gas you know the feeling.

My car began to heave a few dying breaths, and there was no way I was going to make it to the shoulder. So I prayed that the Lord would just get me out of the slow lane as I turned my flashers on. In a last-ditch effort I jerked the wheel to the right, and angels must have seriously moved my car out of harm's way—I had absolutely no gas left.

There was a small island between the slow lane and a freeway on-ramp, and my car just made it to rest there. There was not even a foot between my car and the traffic passing by on the left. I had a little more room on the passenger's side, but not much.

Still on the phone with my mother, I told her where I was and asked her to come and get me. While I waited for her I realized that I was sitting on the *freeway* with countless cars breezing past me, going at least seventy miles per hour. Their speed caused my car to shake every time they zoomed by. And I thought of Danielle, the girl who never made it home from Bible study.

"I am going to die," I thought. So I began to pray and prepare myself to meet Jesus face-to-face. I thought about my last interactions with those I loved and wished desperately that I had been more loving.

About fifteen minutes later my mom pulled in front of me. When the traffic was clear I climbed over to the passenger's seat and quickly opened that door, got out, and jumped into her car. She and I headed to a gas station for a gas can— but it took a little longer than expected because all of the freeway on-ramps within a five-mile radius of my house were closed due to road construction. We had to drive thirty miles just to get five miles down the street!

During this time I was dating my husband, Michael. I was still in a panic as I was on my way to the gas station, so I called him to tell him about the frightening experience I was having. The poor guy has such a tender heart that he began to worry. I hung up with him as my mom and I pulled into the gas station, only to find that the girl working there knew very little about gas cans. She, of course, tried to help—as did several truckers and some other scary-looking men who were prowling around the gas station at eleven o'clock at night.

Finally we filled the can, and as we were pulling out we spotted a police officer. My mom kindly asked him if he would follow us and use his lights to keep us from being hit by other motorists while we filled the tank in my car. He looked at her like she was crazy, but he agreed. Somehow, though, we lost him on the way back to my car. So my mom and I got out and attempted to fill my tank. I say *attempted* because there was no funnel on this can, and a lot of the gas spilled onto the ground and our feet.

Repeatedly I tried to start the car—all to no avail. A roadside construction worker with a big lit-up sign on his truck pulled up behind us about then. We thought he was offering to help us, but after gawking at us he too sped off without lending us a hand.

Exasperated, we decided it was finally time to call and wake my dad up. Getting back in my mom's car I called him, but because he was in bed and the phone is in the kitchen, I had to yell on the answering machine in an attempt to wake him up. It didn't immediately appear to work, so my mom and I started the detour trek past all of the closed on-ramps in her car again, this time trying to get back to our house.

My dad called back at this point, and I told him the whole story. We picked him up at the house, returned to the gas station and put more gas in the gas can, found a funnel, and headed back to my car. Within minutes my dad had gas in my empty tank. Finally we were able to get in my car, start it up, and drive away.

Only later that night, when I got home, did I really begin to see the analogy to our spiritual lives in that story. Often we travel through life with the gauge on our love meters fluctuating up and down at rapid speeds. Sometimes—without warning—our love tanks hit empty, and

Our first response is to turn to everyone but God.

we simply stop in the middle of the road. And our first response is to turn to everyone but God to help us fill our tanks once again.

TRYING TO FILL OUR LOVE TANKS WHEN THEY RUN DRY

Just like I sought help from my mom, my boyfriend (who wasn't even in the country at the time), the gas station lady, truckers filling their gas tanks, a police officer, and a construction worker, we usually turn to other people to fill our love tanks when they run dry.

But even when they all give their best efforts, our tanks are still empty and we are still broken down on the side of the road with the world passing us by at breakneck speeds. Life is hopeless—and dangerous—until we call on our heavenly Dad to come and rescue us from the mess we've made. Thankfully, though, when we choose to call on God, we don't have to awaken Him from a deep sleep like I had to do with my earthly dad.

Psalm 121:3 says, "He who keeps you will not slumber." That's quite encouraging when you realize that 1 Corinthians 16:14 says, "Let *all* that you do be done in love" (emphasis mine). We are to love others *every* hour of *every* day. That means we are never to let our love tanks get empty. But if you are anything like me, your attitudes of self-sacrifice and service are short-lived.

Yes, you have weeks when you gladly do the dishes for your mom, walk your dog named Floppy so he is not cooped up in the house on a rainy day, donate your allowance to sponsor a child through World Vision, teach a children's Sunday school class, write all of your friends encouraging notes, and sing on the youth group worship team. But a day or two into that dream world you wake up, wanting to scream, because you feel as if you are trapped in a nightmare.

What about me? Your mind is flooded with questions. *If I am out meeting the needs of the world, who is going to meet my needs? My love tank is empty!* And you are just an accident waiting to happen, like I was on the freeway. What do we do with our empty love tanks? What can we do to prevent our love tanks from getting empty in the first place?

John chapter 21 gives us deep insights into the lives of two men who learned to love—one who learned to love well, and another who simply learned to love. I'm talking about the disciples known as John and Peter.

Let's look at verses 1–8.

> After these things Jesus manifested Himself again to the disciples at the Sea of Tiberias [also known as the Sea of Galilee], and He manifested Himself in this way.
>
> There were together Simon Peter, and Thomas called Didymus, and Nathanael of Cana in Galilee, and the sons of Zebedee, and two others of His disciples.
>
> Simon Peter said to them, "I am going fishing." They said to him, "We will also come with you." They went out, and got into the boat; and that night they caught nothing.
>
> But when the day was now breaking, Jesus stood on the beach; yet the disciples did not know that it was Jesus.
>
> Jesus therefore said to them, "Children, you do not have any fish, do you?" They answered Him, "No."
>
> And He said to them, "Cast the net on the right-hand side of the boat, and you will find a catch." They cast therefore, and then they were not able to haul it in because of the great number of fish.
>
> That disciple therefore whom Jesus loved [John] said to Peter, "It is the Lord." And so when Simon Peter heard that it was the Lord, he put his outer garment on (for he was stripped for work), and threw himself into the sea.
>
> But the other disciples came in the little boat, for they were not far from the land, but about one hundred yards away, dragging the net full of fish.

Peter was a disciple with an empty love tank. Just shortly

before this seaside meeting took place, Peter denied Jesus. In an hour of darkness, in an hour of great need, Peter had not only failed to love his friend—he had failed to love his Lord. Not once but three times Peter denied that he even knew Jesus. His love tank wasn't just empty—it was bone dry. Had he been driving down the freeway of life, he wouldn't have even had enough gas to sputter over to the shoulder.

No matter what you have done in your life, you couldn't have been more unloving than Peter. Peter dropped the ball on loving a lot, and in our Lord's darkest hour he failed miserably. Yes, there were many periods when Peter did love the Lord every hour of every day. But this time he let his tank get empty. He forgot how much he was loved. He neglected to realize that Christ was laying His life down for him. And because of that, Peter was unwilling to lay his life down for Christ. Later, though, when Christ was risen and had ascended into heaven, Peter refueled his empty love tank and lived the remainder of his life on full. He even went on to die a martyr's death. He couldn't have done that on an empty love tank.

Returning to Old Loves

In John 21, when Peter's love tank is still empty, we see him on the Sea of Galilee returning to an old love: fishing. Before he met Jesus, fishing was Peter's passion.

Peter was doing something similar to what I did on the freeway when I sought help from my mom, my boyfriend, the police officer, and the truck drivers. He was looking for something else to fill his love tank. After he messed up and denied the Lord, he looked for something familiar to return to in order to give him a sense of worth.

Has your love tank been empty recently? Have you fallen short of fulfilling Jesus' command to love every hour of every day? Who—or what—do you use to try to fill your love tank?

I'm not faulting Peter here for going back to fishing. I probably would have done the same thing in his situation. In moments of great failure and loss we all attempt to cling to things that are familiar to us. But the part of this story that redeems Peter is found in verse seven. "And so when Simon Peter heard that it was the Lord, he put his outer garment on (for he was stripped for work) and threw himself into the sea."

Peter, the disciple who had only loved a little—and then didn't love at all—saw the Lord for one of the first times after his denial, and what did he do? He dove headfirst into the water and swam one hundred yards to be with Jesus. He couldn't wait to see Him.

Nothing else mattered. Not their huge catch of fish that was most likely going to make Peter and the other disciples a significant sum of money. Not even all of Peter's friends who had been in the boat with him. None of that was even a thought in Peter's mind when he saw Jesus standing before him once again.

Peter could not get to Jesus fast enough. He was a desperate and broken man. How passionately have you been trying to get to Jesus lately?

Later in that chapter we read that Jesus restored Peter there on the beach that day. But we will save that portion of the passage for another chapter because that carries a whole other lesson in itself.

KNOWING YOU ARE LOVED

For now let's look at John, the author of the very book that tells us this story. Look at how John describes himself in John 21:20: "Peter, turning around, saw the disciple whom Jesus loved following them; the one who also had leaned back on His breast at the supper, and said, 'Lord, who is the one who betrays you?'"

Verse 24 confirms that John is talking about himself here. But think about that for a moment. Instead of simply saying, "Peter turned and saw me" or "Peter turned and saw John," it says Peter turned and saw the disciple whom Jesus loved, the one who had leaned on Jesus' breast. John was known as the disciple who loved. In fact, Jesus saw such an incredible depth of love in John that He entrusted the care of His mother to John when He was on the cross being crucified (John 19:26–27). If Jesus wouldn't be around to care for Mary, John was the next best thing. It was common for John to operate on a full love tank. After all, he was the "beloved disciple."

In 1 John 4:7–8 he tells us: "Beloved, let us love one another, for love is from God; and everyone who loves is born of God and knows God." He's also the one who told us in John 3:16 that "God so loved the world, that He gave His only begotten Son, that whoever believes in Him should not perish, but have eternal life."

The verses John mentions on love are countless. I could go on for pages recounting them. John was a disciple who operated on a full love tank, and it was evident. Why was it that John's tank was so full when Peter's was often so empty? They spent the same amount of time with Jesus.

John was a disciple who loved because he knew how much he was loved. Early on—commentators and theologians say when he was just a teenager, not older than fifteen or sixteen—John learned the art of leaning back on Jesus' breast. He learned the art of intimacy with Christ, always going straight to the Lord to fill his love tank. And when people asked him who he was, he answered, "I'm the disciple Jesus loves."

Knowing that—and basking in it—kept John's love tank full. And with a full love tank he was able to love others more effectively. Those who know how much they are loved love much. Do you know how much *you* are loved?

Maybe someone has hurt you very badly recently and your love tank isn't just empty—it's mangled to the point where it won't hold any fuel. Perhaps your disappointment and grief is so intense that no one even knows it is there. It hurts so badly you don't want to share it.

Maybe you are trying to brush your pain off by telling yourself that it really isn't that big of a deal. But you know what? If it's a big deal to you, it's a big deal to God. He looks down from heaven and sees the needle on your love gauge rapidly declining—and He knows what will happen when you hit empty. He is standing before you desperately desiring to pour into you and fill your tank to overflowing so that you can love Him, and others, every hour of every day.

People can be great tools in the hand of God to remind us we are loved. But when people don't come through for us, God is still crazy about us. Put this book down for a minute and go look in the mirror. Take a good, long look at yourself. Scrutinize every last detail.

That sight just took God's breath away. You captivate God. He is madly, truly, and deeply in love with you. For God so loved *you*, that He gave His only begotten Son.... Maybe, though, you feel like Peter. Your love tank is empty and you have nothing left to give. The remedy for that is found in diving in like Peter to get to Christ faster, and then leaning against Christ's breast like John. *Recognize* that you are the beloved of God. *Identify* yourself as the beloved of God. *Bask* in the knowledge that you are the beloved of God.

> *He is madly, truly, and deeply in love with you.*

Cling to verses like Zephaniah 3:17, which says, "The Lord your God is in your midst, a victorious warrior. He will exult over you with joy, He will be quiet in His love, He will rejoice over you with shouts of joy."

Imagine that! God rejoices over you with shouts of joy! Some translations say He sings over you—that is far better than any love song we could ever hear on the radio. Even when the world ignores you, and no one else even seems to notice you, God notices and He loves you.

Grab a pen and a piece of paper, or a three-by-five card, and write down a verse or two that reminds you that you are the beloved of God. Stick it somewhere you will see it every morning when you start your day—the mirror in your bathroom or your school notebook can be good places. Remind yourself every morning, and countless times throughout your day, that God loves you. Let Him fill your love tank, because He is the only One who can truly satisfy.

When I taught this chapter to my girls' Bible study group, I gave them each a peach rose to remind them of God's love for them. I figured every girl likes to get flowers. What I didn't count on, however, was the depth of the response those roses would invoke in the girls. The following week several of the girls told me they had placed their roses in vases and put them where they could see them often. They said it was a great reminder of God's love for them and helped them keep their love tanks full so they could give out to others. Look for something you can use to remind you of God's love for you, and help fill your love tank. Trust me, having a full love tank does wonders for your perspective.

Once the meter starts to climb on your love gauge, you will find that you have more love to give out to those around you. Those who know how much they are loved are able to love much.

You are the beloved of God. So go out and love that way.

FOR FURTHER THOUGHT:

1. Would you currently describe your love tank as empty or full? How did it get that way?

2. Do you view yourself as someone who is loved or unloved? Why? How does that affect the love you are able to give to others?

3. What are some verses that you hold on to when you feel unloved or low?

4. What are some practical ways to keep your love tank full?

5. What are some ways you can help others keep their love tanks full?

LOVE IN ACTION:

Write three encouraging notes to friends or family members. Write out a verse, reminding them how much God loves them. And let them know you do too. Stick them in the mail or hand-deliver them right away. Your words of encouragement may come at just the right time. Make sure to include verses though. Knowing you love them is encouraging, but knowing *God loves them* is life changing.

6

Keeping It Real

In college I knew this guy who used to hate it when someone would ask, "Hey, how's it going?" and then keep walking without waiting for a response. He said it felt like the other person was giving him a prerecorded greeting instead of a sincere hello.

One day he told a group of us that he usually always stops and waits to see if the person will realize he hasn't answered, or if they will just keep going. About a month or so later I was speed-walking across campus, late for class, moving so quickly I was almost in a slight jog—and I saw this guy walking toward me.

"Hey, how's it going?" I didn't slow down as I called out the greeting over my shoulder. A few feet later I realized what I had done, turned, and saw my friend standing there looking at me. He gave me a slight grin and a head nod.

"Good, and you?" Only after I had responded did he turn back around and continue on his way. So many times we go through life giving other people prerecorded messages—automated love—instead of the real thing. Believe it or not, people *do* know the difference.

How do they know the difference? The real thing is so incredible that nothing else compares. John 15:13 says, "'Greater love has no one than this, that one lay down his life for his friends.'" Wow! That's a pretty high standard. No wonder our cheap imitations pale in comparison.

Most of the time we are not even willing to give people five minutes of our valuable time, much less give them our lives. If love doesn't cost something, it's not the real thing. That's what keeps it real. First Corinthians 13:8 tells us that love does not fail. That means it does not stop. John 13:1 tells us that "Jesus . . . having loved His own who were in the world, loved them to the end."

In other words, He loved the people in His life until His very last breath. He loved them completely. Do you love the people in your life to the end? Or do you eventually give up and quit loving them?

As girls, it seems almost natural for us to turn our backs on those who wrong us and abandon those who stop meeting *our* needs. Growing apart from our friends as we get older is one thing, but dropping them like a hot potato is quite another. Growing apart is usually a peaceful parting of ways, while the other is similar to a painful breakup.

Recently I had dinner with an old friend from high school, someone I hadn't seen in years. It was fun to catch up and reconnect, and it seemed just like old times. But a year or so ago I went to dinner with a friend who had dropped me for a certain guy. They had since broken up, and she wanted to restore our friendship. That dinner was not as comfortable as the other because there was a lot more pain to work through. Make it a point in all of your friendships not to burn bridges if you do choose to move on. You can still love people from a distance.

Actually, we do ourselves a great disservice when we fail to realize that love manifests itself in many different forms. It can be shown through sincerity, having concern for others, being humble in our interactions with others, and being transparent with our feelings. Love can be demonstrated in so many ways that this book could not possibly contain all of them. But we are going to look at a few. Let's look a little closer at some of the things mentioned earlier.

NOT AFRAID TO GET DIRTY

I've always found John 13:1 to be an interesting verse because of the story that follows it. Verses 1–4 say:

> Now before the Feast of the Passover, Jesus knowing that His hour had come that He should depart out of this world to the Father, having loved His own who were in the world, He loved them to the end.
>
> And during supper, the devil having already put into the heart of Judas Iscariot, the son of Simon, to betray Him, Jesus, knowing that the Father had given all things into His hands, and that He had come forth from God, and was going back to God, rose from supper, and laid aside His garments; and taking a towel, He girded Himself about.

Here we see Jesus, the Lord of all, stooping down to assume a position of humility. In an act of love He elevates His disciples to a higher position. Verses 5–17 say:

> Then He poured water into the basin, and began to wash the disciples' feet, and to wipe them with the towel with which He was girded.
>
> And so He came to Simon Peter. He said to Him, "Lord, do You wash my feet?"
>
> Jesus answered and said to him, "What I do you do not realize now, but you shall understand hereafter."
>
> Peter said to Him, "Never shall you wash my feet!" Jesus answered him, "If I do not wash you, you have no part with Me."
>
> Simon Peter said to Him, "Lord, not my feet only, but also my hands and my head."
>
> Jesus said to him, "He who has bathed needs only to wash his feet, but is completely clean; and you are clean, but not all of you."
>
> For He knew the one who was betraying Him; for this reason He said, "Not all of you are clean."
>
> And so when He had washed their feet, and taken His garments, and reclined at the table again, He said to them, "Do you know what I have done to you?
>
> "You call Me Teacher and Lord; and you are right, for so I am. If I then, the Lord and Teacher, washed your feet, you also ought to wash one another's feet.
>
> "For I gave you an example that you also should do as I did to you.

"Truly, truly, I say to you, a slave is not greater than his master; neither is one who is sent greater than the one who sent him.

"If you know these things, you are blessed if you do them."

Back in Jesus' day the feet were the dirtiest, most vile part of a person's body. People walked everywhere they went on sandaled feet through dusty dirt roads. Think about how filthy your feet would be if you ran barefoot around a baseball diamond in that powdery, cakey dirt—then magnify that a hundred times. That's disgusting. *What does this have to do with keeping it real?* Real love is not afraid to get dirty.

Real love is not afraid to get dirty.

By the time this book comes out, my husband and I will have thirteen nieces and nephews (as I write this, we have ten with three on the way). And on several occasions I have watched my sisters-in-law and my brothers-in-law change absolutely disgusting diapers and wipe off muddy or messy children without even batting an eye. They love their children, and because of their love they can do things that even close family members would cringe at—things like changing diapers and giving baths—without thinking twice about it. They just do it. Willingly and lovingly they do it. Most of the time we are not as willing to embrace the dirty and hurtful places in our friends' lives.

THE THREE MEN AT YOUR TABLE

In verse 23—which we did not read—it tells us that John was there with Jesus that night. In the last chapter we talked a little bit about John. He was known as the disciple who loved, and loved much. He was faithful, so he was probably easy to love. Although John was even more loving at the end of his life, we have to assume he was already headed well down that path here on this night. He and Jesus were close. John had just spent all of dinner reclining on Jesus' breast.

Jesus probably *delighted* in washing John's feet. After all, John 13:23 tells us that John was the disciple whom Jesus loved. And we all delight in doing things for those we love. Think about the Johns in your life. Does your heart get excited at the thought of doing something nice and thoughtful for them? Do you get butterflies and warm fuzzy feelings in your stomach as you think of surprising these people with things they really want or need?

Do you have a habit of dropping everything in your life when these people want or need something from you? Do you enjoy every moment you get to spend with them—even if it's just on the phone? Loving the Johns in our life is easy. We delight in it; we take joy in it. And many times the Johns in our life love us back with the same fervor. It becomes a give *and take*, not just a give, and that motivates us to love them even more.

Let's look at someone else who was at that table in the Upper Room with Jesus that night. In the last chapter we also talked about Peter. He wanted to love well—his intentions were always good. But Peter had one fatal flaw: He wasn't loyal. When push came to shove, Peter was more concerned about himself—and his own well-being—than he was about those whom he said he loved.

Think with me for a moment about the Peters in your life. These are people who stick by you most of the time, as long as it's convenient for them. Most of the time you are getting along great with them, you enjoy their company, and you guys are close. But these people have also let you down, disappointed you, and hurt you when it really mattered. You still love these people, but there is a little sting when certain memories come to mind.

Washing their feet probably isn't as easy. You may delight a little less in doing loving things for them. But still, just like the Johns in our life, the Peters come to the table as well. And we are commanded to love them.

There was also another person who stood out at the table with Jesus that night. His name was Judas. He sold his friendship with the Lord for thirty pieces of silver. Think with me about the people like that in your life. They probably come to mind a little too quickly, especially if the wound is fresh. These people are hard to love, because we find it hard to even look at them. Washing their feet would be nearly impossible. Kneeling before them would be too humbling. Touching their dirt would nauseate you. Being their servant would absolutely kill you.

Here we have a full table—John, Peter, Judas, and Jesus. And what did Jesus do? Even though John had not yet fully grown into the disciple of love, and Peter's denial of Jesus was just hours away, and Judas was already in the process of betraying Him, the Lord knew all of that and continued to love them.

Loving All of Them the Same

There's love, and then there's *real love*. Jesus kept His love real in this passage. He took a towel, girded himself, and washed the feet of John, Peter, and Judas alike. Later on that evening, when Jesus reveals that one of the disciples will betray Him, none of the disciples can figure out who it is.

He treated them all the same.

Imagine that! That must mean that when He washed their feet, He treated them all the same. John didn't get an extra massage, Peter didn't get a few sharp squeezes to remind Him to stay faithful, and Judas wasn't passed by—even though Jesus' blood was soon to be on his hands. That's keeping it real. Everyone gets the same measure of love from you—even on bad days.

Jesus was about to tell His disciples that He would be betrayed and crucified, but He took time out to wash their feet. In His humanity, don't you think Jesus' mind must have been racing that night? Don't you think He had more *important* things to do than wash the feet of other people—people who were His *servants*? Jesus was better than them. In weak moments these men *hurt* Him, *ignored* Him, *betrayed* Him, and *forgot* Him.

And yet Jesus washed their feet. He went straight to the

dirtiest part of them and made them clean. You have a John, a Peter, and a Judas in your life. You may have more than one of each. Now the call stands before you: "If I then, the Lord and the Teacher, washed your feet, you also ought to wash one another's feet" (v. 14). "If you know these things, you are blessed if you do them" (v. 17).

But Shannon, you might be thinking, *I'm better than them.*

So was Jesus.

I deserve better from them.

So did Jesus.

They need to learn their behavior is not acceptable.

So did Peter and Judas.

But if I love everyone the same, those I really love will get shafted because I will be giving other people the same amount of love.

Do you think anyone in that room could have possibly felt shafted the night Jesus their Lord washed his feet? I don't think so. Not a single one of the twelve could have felt unloved after an experience like that. Loving others does not diminish your love for those you love more. It just multiplies your love to include more people.

Jesus' love was the real thing. In order to keep our love real too, we must imitate the example He has set before us. We are to love those He has put in our lives, and love them to the end. We are to love each of them, *all* of them, with everything we've got. When you put this book down and close its cover, you will have to face your John, your Peter, and your Judas. Many times treating them all correctly involves examining ourselves and preparing to love them before we actually have to interact with them face-to-face.

CLEANING YOUR HEART OUT

Your John, your Peter, and your Judas have each been divinely placed by God in your life as a tool to make you more like Him—to make you more of the real thing in your style of loving. Don't take a prerecorded version of love and give it to your Judas and your Peter. And don't try to fake it so they, and others, think that you are really loving them.

Don't hide your heart. If you have hurt or bitterness toward your Peter or your Judas, admit it. Don't fake it. Don't love on the outside and hate or hurt on the inside. Come clean to God. Tell a friend who can help you to pray through the issue.

Do whatever it takes, but whatever you do make sure to *deal with it*. Deal with your anger and your hurt. Otherwise, all attempts you make at applying this chapter to your life will fail. You cannot keep it real if you are not going to be real about how you feel. And in all honesty, you cannot truly love John if you hate Peter or Judas. In fact, you cannot even love God if you hate Peter and Judas.

First John 2:10–11 says: "The one who loves his brother abides in the light and there is no cause for stumbling in him. But the one who hates his brother is in the darkness and walks in the darkness, and does not know where he is going because the darkness has blinded his eyes."

Part of keeping it real involves forgiving other people—even when they do not ask for forgiveness. The late Henri Nouwen once said, "Forgiveness is to allow the other person not to be God."[1]

Each of us has our own set of hurts and our own trio of people we need to learn to love, even if we don't want to. We'll never grow if we can't learn to love Peter and Judas the way we love John. But we can't genuinely love them until we clean our hearts out. What have you been hiding in your heart lately? What has prevented you from keeping it real? Who in your life is like John, Peter, and Judas? Have you loved them all with the same love?

If not, what's holding you back? Fear, pain, anger, pride? Dispose of it! Bring it before the Lord and offer it up. That's important because only then can you keep it real.

And when you come to the table of other people's lives, would they classify you as a John, a Peter, or a Judas? What can you do to work on that? Although we all have people in our lives that are unworthy of forgiveness—unworthy of having their feet washed—we need to remember that we were unworthy of God's forgiveness.

Find a way to wash the feet (not literally, of course) of your John, your Peter, and your Judas. Find something that you can do to reach out in love to those you have a hard time loving. It may not be easy; I'm sure washing the dirty feet of unfaithful men was not the easiest task for Jesus. Reach out in love to those who come to the table in your life. And when you do it—mean it. Keep it real.

FOR FURTHER THOUGHT:

1. Identify your John, Peter, and Judas (not out loud, if you are in a group setting). Do you treat them all differently?

2. Which of them is the hardest for you to love? Why?

3. Are you a John, a Peter, or a Judas? How do you know?

4. Do you have bitterness or jealousy in your heart that you need to clean out? How can you do it?

5. What are some ways you can "wash the feet" of your John, Peter, and Judas?

LOVE IN ACTION:

Find a way you can "wash the feet" of your John, Peter, and Judas. Reach out to each of them in love. Treat them all with equal value and respect. Be there for your Peter when she needs you even if she hasn't always been there for you. Let her cry on your shoulder. Stick up for your Judas if you see someone wronging her. Sure, she hasn't stuck up for you, but be a friend to her anyway. As far as loving John goes, this one should be easy. Do something nice for your best friend. Write her a note or buy her a little gift just to let her know how much you appreciate her. Do all of these things without expecting anything in return. Be a true example of love to all of those around you. And when you get frustrated and would rather not do the right thing, think of Jesus washing the feet of unworthy men. He can help you to *keep it real*.

Notes

1. Henri Nouwen, "Moving from Solitude to Community to Ministry," *Leadership* magazine, Spring 1995, 84.

7

Have No Fear

I was only three years old the first time I had my heart broken. Too young to fully understand what was going on, all I knew was that Daddy had moved out for a while. During this time I lived with my mom and grandparents, occasionally visiting my dad on weekends. After about a year my parents reconciled. The process of reassembling the pieces of a broken family was tedious, time consuming, and sometimes downright hard for all of us.

The scars from my parents' separation were ones I would carry with me for life. As a young child I worked hard in school and threw myself into excelling in extracurricular activities in hopes of making my dad glad that he had come back home. My life was a quest to make my father proud.

He was a great dad, bringing flowers to my dance recitals, taking me to the batting cages to work on my swing, having me read to him at night so I could read at more advanced levels, helping me with my math homework (something I never seemed to understand), and just being actively involved in my life. We went on family vacations, had fun holiday traditions, and looked like the all-American family to anyone who watched from the outside.

But deep inside of me, the little girl who used to go and hide under the dining room table and cry her eyes out still resided. Part of me became deathly afraid of being left alone or rejected. Even though my parents reconciled, I still felt vulnerable. The divorce rate was rapidly increasing all around me, and many of my friends came from broken homes.

What if my dad leaves again? What if I marry a man who leaves me? My mind used to race with questions like that, keeping me awake into the late hours of the night. Early in my high school career I made up my mind that I was not ever going to be left with nothing—even if one day I was left by someone I loved. I worked hard in high school so I could get into a great college, and I worked hard in college to get a degree. All that hard work was partly a result of my own ambitions, and partly because I wanted to have a means of supporting myself.

I never wanted to be dependent on anyone else or left to pick up the pieces of a broken heart. Eventually my fear of rejection became a simple quest for independence. I didn't want to *need* somebody else, but more than anything in this world I wanted to be *loved* by someone else. For a long time, though, I pushed that desire aside and focused on other things.

Then, when I wasn't really looking, I fell in love with an awesome and godly man. But loving someone else opened up a lot of old wounds—wounds I thought had healed long ago.

As you know by now, when I first began dating my husband, he was signed up to leave the country to study in Israel for a semester. Two months into our relationship he boarded a plane with a promise to write and call. My heart hurt worse then than it had in years. Once again, I had been left—or at least it seemed that way in my mind. Some days the devil threw a parade and stomped all over my insecurities, stirring up big clouds of fear that almost engulfed me. *What if Michael meets someone else? What if he falls in love with the independence he experiences while he is on the other side of the world, away from me?*

Michael was faithful to write and call as often as he could, and about one month into his trip, when he was finally settled in, I began to hear from him daily. But even with daily phone calls my heart raced and I had to fight fear. Some days I was victorious; other days I was a sobbing puddle. Finally I had to "go back" to my childhood and the pain that first broke my heart to get some answers. I had to ask myself why I was so afraid of being abandoned. After all, my dad had come back home, and my family had remained intact.

AFRAID TO LOVE

Have you ever been afraid of something? I'm not talking about being afraid of the dark or monsters under your bed when you were six years old. I'm talking about being afraid of people and relationships. In one of my classes in college we learned that the number-one fear of Americans is public speaking. Why? Because we are afraid of rejection.

Surprisingly, many studies show that there are more people afraid of public speaking than anything else—even death. There are tons of Web sites and books devoted to the topic. How absurd is that? We care more about what a room full of people will think of our speaking abilities than we care about what will happen to us when we die. Although it manifests itself differently in all of us, rejection is what we fear most. Some of us recoil from those around us for that very reason.

Rejection is what we fear most.

Other people attempt to overcompensate for their fear of rejection by working harder at being liked. In high school I met a girl who knew she would never be a beauty queen, so she made sure she became the best class clown any of us had ever seen. Humor and wit gained her acceptance, and because of that she relied on those traits to make friends. She felt she always had to be funny in order to be loved.

Rejection. What a horrible word. It sneaks into our lives in so many different ways, but it hurts the same every time. A cute guy at school starts paying attention to you, and your heart beats wildly at the thought of him. But a few weeks later he has moved on to someone else. It stings, yet you go on. You run for class president or homecoming court and you narrowly lose the race; the reality sets in that you simply did not get enough votes. Again your heart hurts, but somehow you manage to go on.

You slave over the application and finally apply to the college of your dreams, and they send you a letter in the mail thanking you for your time but informing you that there were simply other students they were more interested in this year. You are crushed, but you pick up the broken pieces and try again. You try out for a spot on a sports team, working out every day and giving it your all, but when the final roster is posted on the locker room wall, your name is not there. Your dreams are dead, but life goes on.

Each time we are faced with rejection, it stings a little longer and the pain is a little more intense because it touches an old wound. Almost every fear out there stems from the fear of being rejected or left alone. Even the dark is not as scary when you have someone to face it with you. But what about when you have to go it alone and face your fears head on?

REJECTION AS A WAY OF LIFE

No one could ever be more afraid of rejection than a leper. Leprosy is a contagious disease that attacks not only someone's outward appearance, but also the bones, marrow, and joints of a person. It begins by appearing as small bumps or spots on the skin, and it eventually eats away at the flesh until fingers, teeth, and even arms and legs begin to rot and fall off. It's painful, disfiguring, and highly contagious.

Back in Jesus' day, at the first signs of leprosy a person would lose all he or she had. Because it is so contagious, all lepers were forced out of their homes and towns—away from their friends and family—and into a leper colony. This was not a temporary thing—it was permanent. These people could not see their friends and family again—ever. The only people they had contact with were other lepers, who most of the time didn't even resemble ordinary people.

Imagine that: A spot shows up on your arm one day in the shower, and in an instant you lose your friends and family, your home, the ability to hug and kiss and hold hands with anyone, your appearance, your health, and everything you own—forever.

Those who lived in leper colonies were miserable and lonely. Their nostrils must have burned with the stench of rotting flesh—theirs and that of the other lepers surrounding them. Those who knew them and loved them lived somewhere out beyond the colony walls and weren't allowed to visit. To those who loved them, lepers were as good as dead. There weren't even phones back then, so there were no holiday or birthday phone calls. There was nothing familiar. No friendly voices, no laughter echoing through the halls. For a leper there was no longer any sense of belonging or acceptance.

On days when a hug would have meant the world, all a leper could do was look down at his or her own rotting flesh and be disgusted. No one was even willing to cleanse a leper's wounds for fear of being infected themselves. Most of us long to have someone make us chicken soup when we get the sniffles. Imagine having to clean out your own rotting and oozing sores! Pain always hurts worse when you feel all alone.

There was no youth group or Friday night high school football games for those in the leper colony. Prom wasn't even worth dreaming about, and being loved by anyone was virtually impossible. Lepers had to go a lifetime without ever being touched. There was no one to rub their head, hug them, cuddle with them, or lean in close and whisper a secret in their ear. There was nobody to even accidentally bump into them. The harsh reality of a leper's life was that no one wanted to be anywhere near him.

If lepers ever considered hiding their wounds and sneaking into town, the second they were recognized people would begin shouting, "Unclean! Unclean!" How's that for rejection? All you want is to walk down the streets of your old neighborhood so you can look into the windows of your old house and see if your family is okay, and the neighbor boy—the one who used to have a crush on you—begins shouting at the top of his lungs.

"Get away! Unclean! Unclean! Leper! Get away! You're not welcome here!" That's enough to devastate anyone. The hearts of those in leper colonies must have decayed just like their flesh. A person can only take so much devastation and rejection before shutting down. Hope must have rotted away before it could rise to the surface in their lives. Rejection wasn't just a *fear* for them. It was a way of life. Acceptance is what seemed foreign. Love was a mere pipe dream. And healing was out of the question for someone this broken in body and spirit.

I don't think anyone could have been more afraid than the leper we read about in Matthew 8. His story consists of three short verses, but we'll only focus on two. We don't know how long he had been a leper, and we have no idea how he heard that Jesus was in town. But it's safe to assume that his disease had robbed him of a normal life. To some extent this man felt broken, abandoned, and alone. And Jesus was his last hope. He had nothing to lose because he had already lost everything.

Having no dignity left, he ventured into town. Perhaps he tried to disguise himself as he passed by the townspeople; perhaps he did not. But Matthew 8:2 tells us that he came to Jesus and bowed down, saying, "Lord, if You are willing, You can make me clean." He came humbly to Jesus, knowing that there was nothing Jesus *had* to do for him. For all this man knew, Jesus could have begun shouting, "Unclean! Unclean!"

But I am sure this man had heard stories about Jesus healing the sick and raising the dead. For the first time in a long time hope must have risen to the surface in his heart, and in a last-ditch effort this man hurried to Jesus. But notice his approach: He came in humility. He knelt before the Lord and humbly asked to be healed. He did not demand it. This man knew Jesus was capable of healing him, but he also knew that Jesus didn't have to act.

"Lord, if you are willing..." How many of our own "Lord, if you are willing" prayers do we have? How many times has hope died in our own lives, yet in a brief moment it rises to the surface and we dare to be healed and love again?

When we have been hurt by people we loved and trusted, usually the last thing we ever want to do is love and trust again. The independence that marked my life in high school and college was safe. I couldn't be hurt if I didn't open my heart. I didn't have to be afraid of love if I wasn't ever going to love anyone.

Don't get me wrong—I had plenty of friends. But in those relationships I kept most people at a safe distance, refusing to let my guard down.

But then Michael came along, and for the first time ever I wanted to let the walls come down in my life. Not only did I want to be loved by him, I also wanted to love him back. I wanted a life with him, a happily-ever-after life that would require laying down my independence and facing my fears.

Early in my relationship with Michael, my mom told me she thought Mike was the tool God had brought into my life to heal the wounds of my past. His semester trip—the one that took him away for four months—was perfectly orchestrated by God because it caused me to face my fears, not just cover them up. And in the four months Michael was gone I had to wrestle with my insecurities. I had to fight to discern what was reality and what was merely fear. And I had to lean on God harder than I ever had before because, for the first time ever, I was not running away from love. Over the years I had gotten quite good at running away from love. Perhaps you have too.

The Power of Touch

What Jesus did for me was much like what He did for the leper in Matthew 8:3. Jesus reached out and *touched* him, saying, "I am willing; be cleansed." The Bible tells us that immediately the leper was healed. Remember, this was a man who had not been touched in what was probably years. Think for a moment about how good it feels to have someone pat you on the back, give you a hug, or even slap you a high five. This man had experienced none of that. He probably longed to be touched more than we could ever imagine. But he did not come to be touched; he came for healing.

Many times we also come to God asking for healing in certain areas, asking to be set free from our fears. We ask in faith believing that healing will really come, but somehow—just like the leper—we don't realize that healing involves being touched by God. We forget that we serve a God who loves us, who is involved in the intimate details of our lives. Our God is relational and personal.

And when healing comes He not only gives us what we are asking for—healing in our outer body—but also what we are really longing for deep down inside. He gives us value, compassion, and intimacy unlike any we have ever known.

When Jesus looked down at the leper who was kneeling at His feet, He could have simply healed him with His voice. He had been known to heal without touching before, like when He told the paralytic to arise, take up his bed, and walk (Matthew 9:6). But when Jesus looked down at this man, He more than likely saw the fear in his eyes. And looking past the fear, Jesus could also see his pain. He knew that this man didn't just need healing; he needed to be touched.

Being the tenderhearted, intimate, and compassionate Lord that He is, Jesus stretched out His hand and touched the man, saying, "I am willing; be cleansed" (Matthew 8:3). The healing that surged through that man's body the instant Jesus touched him could not have been a healing that only touched the surface. This healing had to shake him to his very core.

Think for a moment about the thrill that rushes through your body when someone you love pats you on the back, gives you a hug, or holds your hand. The first time Michael ever held my hand, my heart jumped into my throat (sometimes it still does). Why? Because touch makes us feel valued and recognized. Touch makes us feel loved. Many times touch is what heals us. In his book *The Five Love Languages*, Gary Chapman writes, "... babies who are held, hugged, and kissed develop a healthier emotional life than those who are left for long periods of time without physical contact."[1]

Children who are adopted from orphanages come to life as they are held, cuddled, and touched by their new parents. Elderly people in nursing homes begin to live again when young people come and visit them, especially when their visits include lots of hugs and pats on the back. Broken hearts begin to become whole again when we let God touch us—both with His Spirit and with the hands of other people.

Perhaps as you read these words you realize that it has been quite some time since you have been touched—both by God and by others. Perhaps you have been touched in the wrong way by those who have taken advantage of you or have physically hurt you. If this is the case, you have more than likely become fearful.

Having our hearts broken once or twice is all it usually takes to make us afraid of love. Maybe your broken heart came at a young age, like mine did. Perhaps healing has never come for you. If you have had a parent or someone else you loved and trusted leave you, then maybe you have a hard time believing that God will not leave you too.

TAKING RISKS

Fear is what happens when we do not deal with our pain. It coats our heart with a thick callus so that we cannot be hurt again. We become fearful and standoffish as a way of protecting ourselves. And we are right—if we do this we can no longer feel hurt or pain. But eventually we cannot feel any joy or love either.

God loves risk because risk involves faith.

Walling ourselves in and hiding in fear are not how we should live our lives. If we choose those methods for living, we are living in defeat. This is not God's intention for His children. In 1 John 4:18 it tells us that perfect love casts out fear. Love necessarily involves risk—you take a risk every morning when you get out of bed and face a new day. But God loves risk because risk involves faith.

The leper who came to Jesus took a huge risk. When he went to Jesus that day there was no guarantee that Jesus would heal him. He probably didn't even let himself dream that Jesus would touch him. No one had touched him in years ... why would the Messiah?

He took a risk that involved faith when he went looking for Jesus, but in the end he found not only Jesus but healing and freedom as well. Loving others, even loving God, is always a risk. It always means opening ourselves up to pain and disappointment. But many times we are surprised by the gentleness of the hand that touches us, and we experience a joy and freedom we have never known before.

What is it that you are afraid of right now? Where is fear blocking you from experiencing love in your life? Who have you been shutting out? Who have you been running from? Kneel before the Lord and humbly ask Him to deliver you from your fear and heal you of your hurts. And knowing our Lord as I do, I can promise you that you will be touched like you have never been touched before.

Be touched, be healed. And then go out and be the tool that God uses to touch and heal others.

FOR FURTHER THOUGHT:

1. Describe an event in your life that has made you afraid to love.

2. Have you fully recovered from that pain? How do you know?

3. What is an area in your life you may still need healing in?

4. Describe the last time you felt as if you were touched by God.

5. How can you be a tool in God's hand to help others heal from their hurts and fears?

LOVE IN ACTION:

Look for someone who has gone unnoticed or "untouched." Make an effort to reach out to her and draw her out of her shell. One caution to keep in mind: Do not reach out in a one-time effort if this is a person you see on a regular basis. That might cause her more pain in the end, if she feels like you reached out to her and then rejected her. Find someone (maybe a friend from a broken home, or a loner at school) you are willing to give time and effort to, and build up that person by showing her that it is safe to love again.

Notes

1. Gary Chapman, *The Five Love Languages* (Chicago: Northfield Publishing, 1995), 103.

8

The Secret

Everyone likes to be in on a secret. There is a certain element of importance that comes from being one of a select few who knows something that everyone else *wants* to know. Some people can't keep a secret, even if they try. Others keep their lips tightly sealed as if their lives depended on it. Depending on the importance of the secret, I usually tend to fall into the first category. I just love spreading good news. I can keep a secret if necessary, but I love to be the one who gets to blurt it all out if I can.

Right now, I have a secret I want to share with you. But first, there is a story I have to let you in on so the secret makes sense. So keep reading (no racing ahead and peeking), and I will spill the beans on one of the greatest secrets I have ever learned.

Shel Silverstein's children's book *The Giving Tree*[1] is a fascinating love story for me, although there is not the least bit of romance in it. It's a book about a boy and a tree. When he was young, the boy would swing on the tree's branches, having the time of his life, which filled the tree with great joy. As the boy got older, swinging became a thing of the past, and since he needed some money, the tree let him take her apples and sell them for some cash. The process goes on and on. The boy needs something, the tree gladly offers to supply it, and the boy goes on his merry little way.

Finally, at the end of the book, the boy is an old man, and he visits his friend the tree one last time. Saddened that she has nothing left to give, the tree (who is now just a stump) apologizes to the boy. Winded from his journey, the now tired old man says that he simply needs a place to rest, and the tree joyfully offers her stump. He then sits down with his old friend, and the tree has officially succeeded in loving the boy with everything she had.

Don't we all wish we had a Giving Tree? In many ways God is our Giving Tree. Day by day, hour by hour, He supplies all of our needs. Many times, like the boy, we simply take without offering thanks, and we keep coming back with more wants and more needs (or sometimes wants that we claim are needs) because we are not yet satisfied. Often, those of us who take the most from God offer the least to others. We complain and grow weary when people seem to "suck us dry."

We're willing to give—but just a little. We are willing to sacrifice—but not too much. We are willing to offer our hand—but not our whole hearts. We are willing to give a dollar—but not our whole wallets. The main difference between God and the Giving Tree is that God never runs out of resources like the tree did. He gives us all He has over and over again, even when we are ungrateful or we don't seem to notice. Like the Giving Tree, God loves to bless those He cares about, but that's where the similarity ends. His giving is so much greater that it is beyond description.

We, on the other hand, could afford to be much more like the Giving Tree. This is not to say that we should allow ourselves to be taken advantage of—like some say the tree was. But our attitude should always be more like the tree's and less like the boy's. Any of us who have given even a little bit of love know that it is easy to tire out and quit very quickly. There's a secret to loving the way God wants us to—unreservedly and without measure.

> *There's a secret to loving the way God wants us to.*

THE GREATEST SECRET OF ALL

Are you ready for this? The secret to loving like the Giving Tree is found in being plugged into a source *greater* than ourselves. That way we are not just a tree—we are a tree rooted in the very source of love itself. That means supernatural love will pump through our veins, leaving us with a constant immeasurable supply. John 15:4–9 explains it like this:

> "Abide in Me, and I in you. As the branch cannot bear fruit of itself, unless it abides in the vine, so neither can you, unless you abide in Me.
>
> "I am the vine, you are the branches; he who abides in

Me, and I in him, he bears much fruit; for apart from Me you can do nothing.

"If anyone does not abide in Me, he is thrown away as a branch, and dries up; and they gather them, and cast them into the fire, and they are burned.

"If you abide in Me, and My words abide in you, ask whatever you wish, and it shall be done for you.

"By this is My Father glorified, that you bear much fruit, and so prove to be My disciples. Just as the Father has loved Me, I have also loved you; abide in My love."

If we abide in Christ we can do anything. *Anything?* Yep. *Even love the girl who cheated in order to beat me for a spot on the team?* Yes. *Even love the boy who had the most embarrassing picture of me placed in the school yearbook?* Even that. *Even love the kids who make fun of me every day for being a Christian?* Now you're catching on. If you abide in Christ you can really do anything—and more importantly, you can *love anyone.* Sometimes that is the hardest thing to do.

First John 4:12b says, "If we love one another, God abides in us, and His love is perfected in us." That should be the goal in each of our lives—to have God's love perfected in us by abiding in Him and having Him abide in us.

So just what does it mean to abide? After consulting a synonym finder, I discovered that *to abide* means to remain, to rest, to conform to, and to keep faithful to. So in the context of 1 John 4:12, we are to conform to the image of Christ, rest in Him, remain in Him, and keep faithful to Him. In essence, it means we are to imitate Christ. Because of the bottomless supply of His grace and mercy, we have access through Him to all the resources we need to keep on loving others. What would be impossible on our own becomes possible because of His power in our lives.

Loving Without the Vine

In junior high there was a very mean group of girls in my class. They made fun of my clothes, they made fun of my faith, they made fun of the way I did my homework—they were absolutely ruthless. Yet they were popular. So for a while I tried to be their friend and simply took the abuse they dished out. After all, everyone wants to be popular, right?

In an attempt to gain popularity we will sometimes morph ourselves into giving-tree-type creatures. We will give and give and give until we have nothing left. This usually leaves us broken-hearted, exhausted, and alone. But that is only because we are loving and giving in our own strength. We are imitating Christ but we are not abiding in Him, so we are operating with only our own *limited* strength. We are not plugged into the vine so we have no source to draw from when we run out of love. Since love is not constantly being pumped into us, it cannot constantly be pumped out of us. When we attempt it on our own we get absolutely nowhere.

That's what happened to me with these particular girls. For two whole years I let them run my life. If they wanted lunch money, I had extra to spare. If they invited me to their birthday parties, I attempted to find the coolest gift ever. I wrote them fun notes in class, hoping to get notes in return. Sometimes it worked; other times it didn't.

There were days when these girls and I seemed close—the best of friends. But it never lasted, and I always came out feeling like the stump at the end of Shel Silverstein's book. I had nothing left to give. The only difference between me and the Giving Tree was that I was not about to let them sit on me—I felt trampled on enough!

During my eighth-grade year I switched classes, so I rarely had to see these girls. But when I did—at lunch and break—they attempted to make my life more miserable than they ever had. They spread rumors about me and made rude comments to me. If I tried to be friendly, they would completely ignore me and try to make me feel stupid. Having absolutely no love left for them on my own, I began to learn what it meant to abide in Christ. Some days I seemed to learn well; other days I didn't do so well.

But on many rough days—days when I just wanted to punch these girls in the face—if I chose to call upon the Lord and plug into the vine, there was love enough to go around. Not the mushy, gushy, butterflies-in-your-stomach kind of love that we so often look for, but the kind of love that helped me bite my tongue when a rude comment came to mind, and helped me turn the other cheek when I really wanted to fight back. Many times God's supernatural love was also accompanied by His great grace, which gave me the strength not to cry in response to their rude remarks until I got home and could cry all alone in my room.

God not only gave me enough love to give out to these mean girls, but He also gave me a sense of His own love toward me, which was overwhelming! In moments when I felt the most unloved by other people—if I chose to plug into the vine by reading God's Word or crying out to God in prayer—the most amazing thing would happen. I became instantly flooded with God's peace as I recognized my value in His eyes. Knowing that the God of the universe loved me more than I could ever imagine removed most (if not all) of the pain I experienced due to being rejected and treated harshly by these girls. Being plugged into the vine just makes us better people all around.

What Jesus said really is true, not that I ever doubted Him. If we abide in Christ, the love of the Father will take up residence in our lives and will help us to love everyone we come across. It will make us more willing to give of our time, resources, and talents.

The Secret to the Secret

However, there's a secret to the secret. Not only do we have to abide in Christ, but we have to *keep* abiding in Him. Day by day it is a choice. Sometimes it is a choice that takes a lot of effort, because it is so much easier to give in and be rude or quit loving altogether.

Every day when you wake up, one of the first things you

need to do is decide whether or not you are going to plug into the vine. Many times we bring weariness, frustration, and heartache on ourselves. We know what to do, but we just don't do it. We think it is so much easier to try to love in our own strength. Oddly enough, though, those of us who openly admit that we only have a little love to give usually expect other people to love us without measure. How backward is our thinking? *Hey, I can love you a little, but you need to love me a lot.*

Sometimes we can acknowledge that we are not plugged into the vine. We feel empty, and we know we do not have a lot of love to give. But instead of plugging into the vine, we plug into other people, expecting them to fill us with enough love to give out to other people. This results in lots of frustration and emptiness—not only in ourselves but also in those from whom we have tried to draw love. If we don't have enough love to go around on our own, our friends and family most certainly don't either! Often we overlook that fact.

When other people love us, and love us correctly, that is merely a reflection of God loving us through them. And when we love others, and love them correctly, that is merely a reflection of God loving them through us. The credit never belongs to us, but we are usually more than willing to take it!

DON'T BE A CHRISTMAS TREE

Every year at Christmastime millions of Americans participate in the good old-fashioned tradition of decorating a Christmas tree and proudly displaying it in their homes. I especially love when people put them in front windows so you can look in and see tree after tree filling windows as you walk down the street. Christmas trees bring so much holiday cheer—and they are the center of many great memories as families participate in decorating traditions year after year.

Some people decorate with tinsel, others with lights. Many use ornaments, a few use garland. Most top the tree off with a star or an angel. But no matter how these trees are decorated, they all have one thing in common: They are all dead. Anywhere from the day after Christmas to sometime after New Year's Day, suburban neighborhoods all across America are lined with trash cans full of wrapping paper and dried-out dead trees waiting for the trash collectors to come and pick them up.

Dead trees can only give so much. Dead trees are not real giving trees, although for a while they may seem like it. And if we are not plugged into the vine—Christ Jesus and His love—then that is exactly what we are. We are dead trees. Perhaps that's where you are at as you read this; you are a dead tree or on your way to quickly becoming a dead tree, and you don't know what to do to stop the process.

> *Dead trees can only give so much.*

Begin by opening your Bible and looking up some verses on love. If God is the source of love, then He must have a lot to say about the topic. We will be more loving when we connect with the source of love himself and ask Him to strengthen us. Put the things He says in His Word into practice. As you spend time praying and reading His Word, ask Him to fill you with His love. Ask Him to show you what love really looks like and how you can put it into practice in your life. Jesus said if we are abiding in Him, we can ask for anything and receive it.

Just as the Giving Tree in Shel Silverstein's story was always there to supply the boy's needs, God will always be there to supply yours. If you are feeling unloved, He'll love you. If you are feeling as if you do not have enough love to give others, He'll give you more than enough love to give away. If there is someone you think you just absolutely cannot love, He'll give you His love for them and let you use it.

If you let Him, God will turn you into your own version of the Giving Tree. But He will never expect you to give on your own. He'll plug you into himself first, and then He'll channel His love through you. When you're plugged into Him you'll be a Giving Tree who never quits. And just like the tree in the children's story, loving others and meeting their needs will bring you great joy.

Love does not give begrudgingly. It does not sigh in irritation before opening its arms wide. Love does not even hesitate; it just lavishly pours forth on the object of its affection. One test of whether you are plugged into the vine or not is whether or not there is joy in your loving. Those who are plugged into the vine always experience joy in their loving because joy comes straight from Jesus himself.

So now you know the secret: Plug into the vine and *stay* plugged into Him, and you will love others the way Christ loves you. Be a Giving Tree that's firmly rooted in the source of love himself, and your love will never go dry. Read God's Word, talk openly with Him about your lack of loving or the frustrations you encounter when you try to do it on your own. Trust me, if you do these things the results will be amazing. Slowly but surely, as you take root in Christ, you will become a healthier and happier "Giving Tree."

People will eventually notice, and they will want to know the secret too. Don't worry—you don't have to keep this secret to yourself. Go out and share it with everyone you can find. After all, that's what being a Giving Tree is all about—loving others and giving love away.

So go and find a friend right now, flash them a killer smile, and simply ask, "Do you want to know a secret?" I can almost guarantee you'll have her full and undivided attention.

FOR FURTHER THOUGHT:

1. In the story of *The Giving Tree*, do you feel more like the boy or the tree? Why?

2. Do you go to God simply to get something from Him, or do you enjoy a relationship with Him? What's the difference between the two?

3. Are there people in your life who view you as a "Giving

Tree"? How do you respond to them? What is your source of strength?

4. Describe what "being plugged into the vine" looks like to you.

5. How can you apply "the secret" to your life?

LOVE IN ACTION:

Take some extra time to read God's Word. Read through the parables and look at the example Jesus set for loving other people. Spend time in prayer, asking Him to give you supernatural love for other people. Then—and only then—go out and put the things you read into action. Love others with the love of Jesus by being plugged into the vine.

Notes

1. Shel Silverstein, *The Giving Tree* (New York, NY: Harper-Collins Publishers, 1964).

9

Lead by Example

A girl stood in the middle of her new Southern California high school campus with tears in her eyes, staring at her schedule as if she thought looking at the foreign room number would cause her to instantaneously appear there.

Her baggy overalls and grandmotherly turtleneck attested to the fact she wasn't from the area. She wore no makeup, and her plain brown hair fell to her waist in a loose braid. She bit her bottom lip and adjusted her large glasses nervously without looking up.

Hundreds of girls with golden tans and long blond hair rushed past her, making her feel as if her childhood Barbies had come to life to haunt her. She began chewing her right thumbnail and shifting her weight nervously.

The Associated Student Body (ASB) president—who was one of those Barbie look-alikes—bumped into the girl, causing her to drop her books on the ground. Without stopping, the president gave the girl a disgusted look and moved on, chatting animatedly with her friends.

A few minutes later the leader of the Christian club came bustling along. "Gotta get to Bible study," she muttered to herself. "Gotta get to Bible study; otherwise I would stop and help." Stepping over the girl, she too passed without offering her hand. Just behind her came the school loner no one really talked to much. He was known to dabble in drugs and partying.

"Can I help?" His voice was gentle as he bent down to pick up her books for her. She pushed her dark-rimmed glasses up her nose with her thumb and studied the boy for a moment. After reading his *Skateboarding Is Not a Crime* T-shirt, she looked down at her own farmlike attire as if to silently ask, "Why would someone like *you* stop to help someone like *me*?"

"Are you new?" He smiled at her when he spoke, his unruly curls poking out from beneath his baseball cap that was worn backwards. When she didn't answer he offered, "Would you like me to walk you to your next class and show you where to go from there?"

As the girl brushed herself off, the boy carried her books and walked her to class. He even offered to meet her by the snack bar line at lunch so she would have someone to sit with, and he would show her around campus afterward. The girl eagerly accepted his offer—after all, he was kind of cute—and the two of them became fast friends.

Yeah right, you might be thinking. But stories like that happen more often that we would like to admit. In fact, some are even recorded in the Bible. *The Bible? The Bible tells stories about farmlike girls and loner boys?* Before you begin to wonder what translation I read, think hard for a moment. The story I just told you is based loosely on a passage of Scripture. Do you recognize it? It is found in Luke 10:30–37. In Sunday school it was taught to us as the parable of the good Samaritan.

> Jesus replied and said, "A certain man was going down from Jerusalem to Jericho; and he fell among robbers, and they stripped him and beat him, and went off leaving him half dead.
>
> "And by chance a certain priest was going down on that road, and when he saw him, he passed by on the other side.
>
> "And likewise a Levite also, when he came to the place and saw him, passed by on the other side.
>
> "But a certain Samaritan, who was on a journey, came upon him; and when he saw him, he felt compassion, and came to him, and bandaged up his wounds, pouring oil and wine on them; and he put him on his own beast, and brought him to an inn, and took care of him.
>
> "And on the next day he took out two denarii and gave them to the innkeeper and said, 'Take care of him; and whatever more you spend, when I return, I will repay you.'
>
> "Which of these three do you think proved to be a neighbor to the man who fell into the robbers' hands?"
>
> And he [the lawyer] said, "The one who showed mercy toward him." And Jesus said to him, "Go and do the same."

First of all we have a Jewish man who is walking along the road from Jerusalem to Jericho. And along the way he is attacked by robbers who take him for all he is worth and leave him for dead.

And along comes a priest. You would think a priest would offer to help in a situation like this. I mean, you can't get much holier than a priest. But no, this priest, much like the ASB president or the leader of the Christian club, sees someone who is hurting, one of his very own people, yet he passes by—too busy to notice or too self-absorbed to care.

Then along comes a Levite. Levites were customarily helpers to the priests. Of the tribe of Levi, they were responsible for making sure the temple was clean and in good working order. I guess you could say the particular Levite in this story was more concerned with cleaning up the outward temple than he was with living a clean and loving life.

And then comes a Samaritan—the most *despised* people group there was at that time. The Jews considered Samaritans their enemies. And just like the outcast in our high school story, the Samaritan stopped and helped this man. Not only did he help him, he also went far above and beyond the call of duty.

Not only did he clean and bandage this guy's wounds, but he also took him to an inn, took care of him all through the night, and then paid for the innkeeper to care for the man until he was better. The Samaritan did not know the Jew; he knew only that the Jews were enemies of his people. He also realized this man would not likely be able to pay him back.

In fact, in coming to his rescue, the good Samaritan probably risked being beaten up himself. If other Jews saw him dragging the mutilated body of this Jew into the city on the way to the inn, they could have easily thought that he was the one who had accosted him. Love costs. If it doesn't cost, it's not the real thing.

Just like the boy in our story, the Samaritan was an unlikely hero. You would have thought that the ASB president or the Christian would have stopped to help the new girl. After all, they were *leaders* on their campus.

Instead, it was the loner that no one really paid much attention to that emerged from the shadows and became someone's knight in shining armor. Think with me for a minute about what could unfold in that girl's life in the weeks and months that followed. Do you think she would want to join the ASB homecoming committee and work with the president? Do you think she would desire to join the Christian club and become fast friends with the girl who was too busy getting to Bible study to help her pick up her books?

Or do you think she just might take a hit off the joint of her new-found friend when he invites her to a party where that kind of stuff is going on? Now some of you may think I am being extreme here. But in all honesty I am not. People follow

> *People follow those who are nice to them.*

those who are nice to them, those who reach out to them, and those who offer *any* form of acceptance to them. I am not stereotyping skaters or loners. And I am not saying that the Good Samaritan had a questionable background. But Samaritans were despised by Jews; they were not known as people with whom you would want to associate. The boy in this story simply serves to illustrate that point.

WHERE HAVE ALL THE GOOD SAMARITANS GONE?

At this time in your life your peers are very vulnerable. Many will follow the path of least resistance—the path that is most welcoming and lined with friendly faces. But most of the time when hurting people seek help, they are met with fake smiles instead.

If we as Christians are always too busy getting to Bible study, or too busy with our own friends to make any new ones, the world will continue to decay around us. We as Christians have a responsibility to love other people. Do you remember what Jesus' closing statement in this account in Luke was? "Go and do likewise." And in John 13:34 He tells us to love "even as I have loved you."

The first story I shared was a compilation of many stories girls have shared with me blended into one. It is a definite worst-case scenario situation. But I came across the true story of a boy named Brian Warner that is powerful as-is. Brian went to a Christian academy all the way through eighth grade. When he got to high school he was the new kid in youth group, and the youth pastor tried to reach out to him a few times, but Brian was just a little bit different from the other kids. He was hard to relate to, so the youth pastor stopped reaching out and Brian stopped coming to youth group.

Years later, a former student of this youth pastor called him to ask him if he knew whatever happened to Brian Warner. When the youth pastor said no, the student informed him that Brian had become very, very famous. Only he wasn't going by the name Brian Warner anymore—the public knew him as Marilyn Manson.[1] Now, I am not saying that it is the youth pastor's *fault* that Brian Warner became Marilyn Manson. In the end we are all responsible for our own actions.

But what I am saying is that *sometimes a little love goes a long way.* Leading by example is all it takes sometimes to save someone from going down a path of destruction. But love costs, and leading by example is not easy.

Don't use your age as an excuse. You don't have to be an upperclassman or a high school graduate before you can lead in showing love. First Timothy 4:12 says, "Let no one look down on your youthfulness, but rather in speech, conduct, love, faith and purity, show yourself an example of those who believe." Sometimes it's the young who lead the old.

LEARNING TO SEE THOSE AROUND YOU

If you are going to be a leader, you have to learn to look at the world with different eyes. You have to look beyond the surface and actually see people for who they really are, deep down inside. Jesus was able to do this beautifully. John 5:1–9 is one of many passages illustrating Jesus' ability to read people.

After these things there was a feast of the Jews, and Jesus went up to Jerusalem.

Now there is in Jerusalem by the sheep gate a pool, which is called in Hebrew Bethesda, having five porticoes.

In these lay a multitude of those who were sick, blind, lame, and withered, waiting for the moving of the waters; for an angel of the Lord went down at certain seasons into the pool, and stirred up the water; whoever then first, after the stirring up of the water, stepped in was made well from whatever disease with which he was afflicted.

And a certain man was there, who had been thirty-eight years in his sickness.

When Jesus saw him lying there, and knew that he had already been a long time in that condition, He said to him, "Do you wish to get well?"

The sick man answered Him, "Sir, I have no man to put me into the pool when the water is stirred up, but while I am coming, another steps down before me."

Jesus said to him, "Arise, take up your pallet, and walk."

And immediately the man became well, and took up his pallet and began to walk.

What is one of the first things you notice about that passage? Did you catch it? "When Jesus saw him..." One of Jesus' greatest strengths was that He *saw* people. And because He saw them, He could touch them, love them, and heal them.

Look also at John 11:33: "When Jesus therefore saw her [Mary] weeping, and the Jews who came with her, also weeping, He was deeply moved in spirit, and was troubled."

Once again, in a moment of need, Jesus *saw*. He saw Mary and He acknowledged her pain. He didn't simply offer a thoughtless pat on the arm or a breezy answer like, "I'm praying for you, girl." He stopped. He stooped. And He took a moment to meet Mary on her level. He did the same with the paralytic. When was the last time you *saw* the people around you? I mean *really* saw them? Someone once told me that if you treated everyone you met as if they were hurting, you would be treating 95 percent of them correctly.

What a powerful statement. But oftentimes we just blow right by people with the "Gotta get to Bible study" mentality of the Christian club leader in our opening story. Leaders recognize that the girl who talks with a funny accent is really trying her hardest to fit in; she can't help it if she has been instantaneously transplanted into a whole new culture.

Leaders recognize that the girl who wears lots of makeup and tight revealing clothing is just looking to be loved. They see all of these things she is hiding behind for what they really are: masks to cover her insecurities. Leaders see that when a friend is being petty, selfish, and mean, it is just her way of responding to the fact that she does not feel as if she is being loved enough.

And leaders can usually be spotted from a distance. They walk just a little differently than other people. Their backs are usually just slightly bent from all of the times they stooped down to help those who have fallen, those who are hurting, and those who need just a little extra tender loving care. Leaders are also those who do not give up and quit when the going gets tough and the loving gets hard.

Bringing Love, Even if You Come Alone

My husband once told me that sometimes God works by the process of elimination. When everyone else bails out, gives up, gives in, and quits, the true leaders are always left standing. And because of this they are able to make an earthshaking impact. Everyone in this world is looking for love. Everybody wants to be loved—absolutely everybody.

Think with me for a moment about the people in your life. They can be family members, close friends, or people you don't really know yet see all the time—like the Starbucks barista you see every morning when you get your latte on the way to school, or the girl you walk by every day on the way to your Spanish class—the one who is always standing alone.

Maybe you have a senior-citizen neighbor who stumbles outside once a day to check his mail—an ordeal that usually takes him about half an hour just to get to the curb and back. Perhaps it's a single mom in your church who could use a baby-sitter so she can have some time to herself, but she cannot afford one. Or maybe it's a good friend who has been a little bit distant lately. You can tell something is going on with her, but you have been too busy to ask.

Who have you been overlooking lately or taking for granted? Who haven't you been *seeing*?

Life is busy—I know. My life is very busy, and I am sure

yours is too. But it's important that we take the time, that we *make* the time, to love other people. Sometimes a simple thank-you to someone who is busy and overworked is enough to make a big difference. Recently someone did a huge favor—unasked—for Michael and me. In return we sent him a box of chocolates as a thank-you. This man was so touched that he sent us a thank-you e-mail for our thank-you gift. He said, "It was nice to be noticed."

Giving of your time, effort, and gifts has everything to do with loving others because we live in a selfish world where very few people are willing to give of themselves and take the time to notice anyone else—much less do anything for anyone else, especially if it costs them something. A few weeks after my girls' Bible study group studied this topic, my friend Sam came to chat with me.

Sam heard me share this message twice. Both times a certain friend came to her mind when I asked the girls whom they had been overlooking in their lives. Sam thought of calling her friend, and resolved to do so. But life got in the way, and Sam got busy. Less than a month later Sam found out the girl was in the hospital because she had tried to commit suicide.

"I know it's not my fault," Sam told me as our friend Liza offered a comforting arm pat. "But seriously, I think a phone call is all it would have taken to make a difference. This girl just felt unloved."

Thankfully, the girl did not succeed at committing suicide, and Sam got a second chance. Not all of us are always that fortunate. We need to take every opportunity we have to love other people. The little things—like phone calls—mean more than we could ever imagine.

The girls in my group are really awesome. They are always doing fun little things for me. Two sisters made me pink beaded earrings because they know I love pink and I love to wear big crazy earrings! They had no clue that the night they gave them to me I was so tired I wanted to be anywhere but at Bible study.

Another time Megan and Ashley—two of the girls in the small group I led a while ago—heard I was sick and went to the store and filled a hot-pink trash can until it overflowed with every possible pink thing made to make someone feel better: tissues, cough drops, cough syrup, gum, a shower scrub, and many other fun little trinkets. The gesture didn't break my fever, but it did cause me to break into a huge smile.

Do you live your life with such fervor? If your friends had to describe you, would they classify you as someone who loves? The little things truly matter. A junior high girl who came in to counsel with me looked at me with tears in her eyes as she told me one of her friends wrote fun little notes in class to everyone else in their circle but her. This seemingly small thing crushed her.

LOOKING BEYOND YOURSELF

Every single person out there wants to be loved more than they are being loved in this moment. Yet many of us are too naïve to notice or too self-absorbed to care. For some reason we cannot get past our own desire to be loved, and as a result we walk around without really loving anyone. Instead, we surround ourselves with only those people we can take from, and not those to whom we can give something.

The true test of whether or not you love someone is if you can still love them in a moment when they can do absolutely nothing for you. A few weeks ago, in my quiet time, I read the first several verses in 1 Corinthians 13 and stopped cold. I think there is power in those verses that is commonly overlooked.

> If I speak with the tongues of men and of angels, but do not have love, I have become a noisy gong or a clanging cymbal.
> And if I have the gift of prophecy, and know all mysteries and all knowledge; and if I have all faith, so as to remove mountains, but do not have love, I am nothing.
> And if I give all my possessions to feed the poor, and if I deliver my body to be burned, but do not have love, it profits me nothing.

Wow! Love is a powerful thing. It is an important thing. In fact, it is *every*thing. Think about that for a minute—if you can speak with the tongues of angels, you can prophecy, you have knowledge enough to know all things, you have faith to move mountains, you have given all you have to the poor, and you have volunteered to have your body burned for the sake of Christ, yet you do not have love, then you have absolutely nothing. That's what Paul says. All your efforts amount to zilch.

What is it again that is making you too busy to reach out and love somebody? What is it that is blinding your eyes so that you cannot truly see those around you? Somewhere in your life there is someone who is hurting, someone who needs love, someone to whom a kind word, a simple phone call, or even a quick note would make her whole week.

Somewhere in your school, or in your youth group, there is someone who has gone all week without being loved—or even noticed. If you are thinking, *Yeah, I am that person,* then I want to tell you I am so sorry. Jesus sees your pain. But if you are hurting right now, you can use your pain to relate to someone else who is hurting too. Don't use it as an excuse to focus all of your attention on yourself and ignore others around you.

If pain isn't your problem, maybe you are just too busy to love others. In that case, let me tell you that life will *always* be busy—and a lot of what we call busy is just plain unimportant stuff. Check your calendar; something needs to give if you are really that busy. Drop a club or an activity, but please—for heaven's sake—don't drop love. If you have too much homework to love someone else, then take a fifteen-minute study break and write a quick note to someone you think could use a little love.

Be a little late to class if that's what it takes to help the lost and lonely girl who is new find her way to class. Chances are, she'll never forget you, and you will forget that tardy before the day is over.

It takes only one person to implement change. The ones who go against the flow are always noticed, and even if they are criticized at first, it is inevitable that someone will eventually begin to follow them. Because being different is a sign of courage, and courage is a sign of a leader. Those who go against the flow can eventually *change* the flow.

Someone has to lead. Most people are followers by nature. If Christians are not imitating Christ and setting an example for others to follow, think of the poor examples that will rise up to lead others astray. One person is all it takes to lead a multitude. The question lies in *which way* the multitude is going to be led.

> *Being different is a sign of courage.*

Are you doing your part? Are you leading in love? Or are you passing through life as a spectator—or even worse, a follower? You can bet that in our self-absorbed world love will stand out. Those who love *will* be noticed. Those who love will be different. Those who are filled with the love of God should be the most loving of all. You are filled with the love of God. What are you going to do with it—give it to the world like He asks us to, or are you going to keep it all to yourself?

FOR FURTHER THOUGHT:

1. In the opening story, are you more like the ASB president, the Christian club leader, or the loner?

2. When was the last time you looked past the surface and really *saw* the needs of someone around you? What did you do in response?

3. Are you a leader in love, or a follower? Why are you that way?

4. Why do we need loving leaders?

5. How can you become more of a leader in your approach to love?

LOVE IN ACTION:

Look for an area of your life where you tend to be a follower, going with the flow, in regard to loving others. Break out of your comfort zone and love others. If you have a hard time talking to those you don't know, start with a smile and a warm hello. Let people know there is a really loving girl hidden behind all of the shyness. If you have great ideas about how your youth group can get involved in the community, yet you are waiting for someone else to implement them, go to your youth leader and see if he or she can help you organize something. Lead in the area of loving.

Notes

1. *www.cyberspacecommunitychurch.com/hisplace/story43.html.*

10

More Than These

I absolutely love the beach. In fact, I'm still sporting a slight sunburn from a relaxing day there last weekend. Nothing is more fun for me than splashing in the waves or feeling wet sand squish between my toes. Living in Southern California, the beach is a place I frequent all year long. Whether it's a cloudy winter morning where I bundle up and sit on the sand watching the fog roll across the water, or a sunny summer afternoon playing Bocce Ball with my husband, God always meets me at the beach.

Not only does He appear in the majesty of the vast ocean and the brilliance of a multicolored sunset, but His presence seems to engulf me when I simply hang out on the shore. When I was in college, two of my roommates and I took a vacation to Maui, and I remember lying on a beautiful Hawaiian beach all alone one afternoon, silently praying to the Lord. When I opened my eyes there was a vibrant upside-down rainbow in the sky above me—it looked like the smile of God. I remember being warmed by God's presence in that moment in a way I will never forget.

The Lord likes to show up on beaches. In Matthew 4:19

we find Jesus walking along the beach when He chooses to call two of His disciples. He tosses a simple invitation their way. "Follow Me, and I will make you fishers of men." The Bible says they *immediately* dropped their nets and followed Him. Peter was one of those to forsake all and pursue the Lord with all He had. Jesus asked for everything on the beach that morning, and Peter willingly gave it.

Think of that for a moment. The Lord asked Peter and His other disciples to give up *everything* they held dear—their jobs, their families, and their homes. Everything that was familiar and comfortable had to be left behind if they were to obey God's call to them. Has He ever asked something similar of you? What would you do if He did? The Lord's words to you are similar to His words to Peter and the other disciples on that crisp morning as they were out getting ready to toss their nets into the Sea of Galilee.

"Daughter," He says to you tenderly, with a smile on His face. "Come, take up your net and follow me." Or perhaps His message to you is a little deeper than that. Maybe God is looking at you and the situations in your life and is simply saying, "Child, take up your *cross* and follow me."

THE DIFFERENCE BETWEEN A NET AND A CROSS

The two commands are very similar but, as we all know, the difference between a net and a cross is huge. Taking up our net means taking up the skills and resources God has given us and using them for His glory. It means as musicians we are to sing for His glory, as writers we are to write for His glory, as athletes we are to play for His glory. It means that we are to follow Him before doing anything else. It means seeking Him *first*.

Taking up our cross, however, means seeking Him *only*. So many times when it comes to loving God, we think we can get away with the minimum. We think we can love God and love everything else just as much. Maybe that works for us in the beginning, but over time it is not enough just to love the Lord. We must come to love Him more than everything else. Sometimes He must strip us of everything else we love so that we can learn this. It can be a hard lesson to learn because we don't like the idea of losing everything in order to gain Christ. We don't realize that Christ *is* everything.

Many times we try to hold on to other things. *I want Jesus, but I still want the freedom to be popular, attend parties, date anyone I want, and live my life how I choose,* we think to ourselves. We like the concept of being saved by grace because grace is free. It doesn't involve our giving anything up. Having a relationship with the Lord, and actively growing in that relationship, scares us because it can be quite costly. Yes, we are saved by grace. But often we grow through sacrifice. Our commitment to Christ will cost us some of the freedom we so dearly prize.

When I married my husband I made a commitment to forsake all others and love him alone. I willingly gave up my freedom to ever date anyone else out of love for him. God requires the same from us. We are to forsake the things of this world, the things that rival God in our hearts. That doesn't mean we have to give up everything—just everything that keeps us from putting God first.

Same Beach, Different Story

For Peter there were times when Jesus asked him to take up his net, and times when He asked him to take up his cross. Three years after He met Peter on the beach and asked him to follow Him, Jesus surprised Peter with a visit on that very same beach. This time it was different; a lot had happened since the day Peter left everything—he had walked with Jesus, talked with Jesus, and spent time in an intimate personal relationship with his Lord. He had witnessed miracles and had even walked on water (just off the shore of that same beach).

But in a moment of weakness Peter, the disciple who had promised to go with Christ to His death, also denied the Lord—not once, but three times. In the past he had taken up his net and followed Jesus. This time he needed to do something more.

When Peter saw Jesus standing on the shore cooking breakfast, as recorded in John 21, I'm not sure if he thought of the day when Jesus first called him to be one of the twelve. But now, as we talked about in an earlier chapter, Peter couldn't wait to see Jesus. He dove into the water and swam the whole one hundred yards to the shore (John 21:7–8).

And when Jesus met him there on the beach, He broke bread with Peter, as He had done many times before, and presented

Peter with a question. Although the question was simple, the answer was anything but simple.

If I close my eyes I can see Jesus and Peter standing on the shore of the Sea of Galilee with the waves crashing in the background and the fish crackling on the fire. Maybe there was even a slight breeze rustling their hair. I see our Lord tenderly looking at Peter as He poses His question in John 21:15: "Simon, son of John, do you love Me more than these?"

Most commentators aren't sure what Jesus was referring to when He said "these." Some say it was the abundance of fish Peter had just caught (symbolizing wealth). Others say it could have been the boats (symbolizing his profession). Most, though, tend to believe the question Jesus was asking was, "Do you love me more than the other disciples love me?"

In Matthew 4 Jesus asked Peter to forsake everything he knew and loved in order to follow Christ, and Peter quickly and firmly responded. In John 21 Jesus was asking the same question, but this time Peter had an idea of how costly it would be if he agreed. In verses 18–19 Jesus seems to suggest that Peter will die a martyr's death.

In the beginning of Peter's walk with Jesus it was enough to simply love Him. But as time went on the Lord required more of him. Peter could no longer simply love Jesus—he had to love Him *more than these*. We don't know what Peter's *these* was, and truthfully it doesn't really matter. What does matter is what *"these"* represents in your life.

WHEN YOUR *THESE* HAS A NAME AND A FACE

Before Michael left for Israel on his four-month adventure, he took me to this passage. Even now I remember the night as if it were yesterday. In one small moment my perspective was changed forever. I could no longer practice loving God more than anything else in theory only. I had to live it out in my life.

"Shannon," he said to me as he squeezed my hand, "what if I am the *these* in your life? What if you are the *these* in mine? What if God has placed us in front of each other and is now asking us, 'Do you still love me? Do you love me more than *these?*'"

I took a deep breath and fought back tears. He was right—he *was* my *these*. I had waited patiently for years for God to bring a godly man into my life. Now here he was, and my heart was happier than it had been in a long time. But this man did not belong to me. I had to let him go. For four whole months we had to keep living out God's call on our individual lives on opposite sides of the world, unsure of how our story would turn out.

Part of me wanted to say, "Lord, you *know* I love you. I have walked with you and served you faithfully for years. Why are you asking me this question? And why are you asking it now?"

There was something very costly sitting in front of me, and the Lord was saying, "Shannon, I know you love me. But do you love me *more* than Michael? Do you love me enough to trust me?" If I answered yes, it changed everything. It meant that I turned to the Lord and gave Him back the gift He himself had given me, leaving me unsure of whether or not I would ever get it back. That was a tough thing to do. Perhaps you know from personal experience.

But imagine my joy when Michael returned from Israel and handed me a heart-shaped pillow made specially for me while he was over there. On the front was a picture of him at the Sea of Galilee—the

If I answered yes, it changed everything.

very same beach Peter was at when Jesus posed His question to him. Above the photo are the words, "Loving you from the Sea of Balilee" (apparently there was a mix-up in the translation). But I got the message just the same. God had asked me to give up my *these*, and when His purpose was accomplished He gave Michael back to me.

What are the things that represent *these* in your life? Is it a person? Is it your popularity? Is it some incredible opportunity? Is it your plan of what you think your life should be? Whatever it is, you must learn to let it go.

Someone once told me that the gifts God gives us are like sand. If we receive sand with open palms, we can actually hold small mountains of it in our hands. But if we try to hold on tight and clench our fists around it, it will slip through the cracks in our fingers and we will be left with nothing.

The only reason the Lord asks us if we love Him more than these is because He wants to keep us focused on the Giver, and not the gifts He brings. When I was in college, we once had a chapel speaker who told us a story about his young daughter. She would come running to him all ready to play each day as he walked through the door, coming home from work.

One night at dinner she asked him for permission to get a kitty. Because this man was a good father and wanted his little girl to be happy, he conceded and bought her a kitty. Several days later when he came home from work, he noticed his daughter didn't come running to him as she always did.

"Sweetie, where are you?" His voice echoed down their long hallway.

"In here," came her muffled little voice. "I'm playing with my kitty." The chapel speaker paused at this point in his story.

"From then on," he said solemnly, "I never liked that cat."

Although there is a hint of humor in what he had to say, there is also a stinging truth buried in that story. As our loving heavenly Father, God delights in bestowing His richest blessings upon us. But, sadly, we often let them distract us from our awesome relationship with Him.

Checking Our Motives

Psalm 37:4 says if we delight in God, He will give us the desires of our hearts. James 1:17 says that every good and perfect gift is from above. And Matthew 7:11 says that if we, as imperfect as we are, know how to give good gifts to our children, then God knows all the more how to lavish His children with rich and wonderful gifts.

Sometimes God asks us for something and will give it back to us in time (as He did in my case with Michael). Other times He asks us to give something up forever (Peter never returned to being a professional fisherman after that fateful day in John 21). But He only does that when He has something better in store for us.

Many times, though, we love God *for* the blessings. We only love Him *until* the blessings come. When times are hard and God is all we have, we cling to Him for dear life. We find ourselves pouring our hearts out in prayer and reading His Word in desperate search of answers to the questions that plague us. But when life gets good and God starts handing out the blessings, we tend to forget where the gifts are coming from, and we fail to offer up more than a cursory "thank you" for what the Lord has done. We may think we love Him "more than *these*" but we really don't.

If that is the kind of love we have for God, then we know nothing of true love at all. God gave us *everything*, so why is it that we flinch at the idea of giving Him *anything*? When I sit and truly ponder the meaning of the word *love*, I always have to go back to the Bible. The message of the Gospel is the very definition of love itself.

True love *is* sacrifice. God gave us the ultimate sacrifice in His Son, Jesus. If our love, whether it is for the Lord or for other people, is genuine, there will be some element of sacrifice and self-denial involved. And more than anything else, loving someone—anyone—is a choice. Love is a verb, an action. It means consciously choosing to put someone else and their interests and desires before your own. And when it comes to loving God, it means laying down your own interests and dreams, and surrendering completely to Him.

Many times, when we are on the brink of some of life's greatest blessings, God will take us through a period of testing. Each of us will have days when God holds our dreams and the very desires of our hearts up in front of our faces, and asks us to surrender them—to give them up and potentially let them die.

"Surrender," He says. "Let go. Trust me." More often than not we wrestle with God when He asks something like that of us. *Why, God?* Our minds race and our hearts plead as we look for any way but the way that is marked out for us. Sometimes we would even be willing to give anything else—if we could keep the one thing God asks of us.

IDOL WATCHING

Job 23:10 says, "But He knows the way I take; when He has tried me, I shall come forth as gold." Perhaps right now you find yourself in a moment of great testing—your knees are weak, your heart is tired, and your body is just plain weary. God is asking for your *these,* He is asking you to love Him more than anything else. Yet you find yourself clinging to the one thing the Lord asks of you. Perhaps your knuckles even hurt from gripping your idol so tightly.

Idol? Did she just say idol? You may find yourself growing defensive at the mention of that term. *I don't have any idols,* you may be thinking to yourself. But if there is something you love more than—or even as much as—God, then you have an idol. And according to Exodus 20:3, that is one of the ten things God will not tolerate.

God is a jealous God, and rightly so. He gave everything in an attempt to win your heart, and He should not have to share it with anyone else. This is not to say that we are not to love other people throughout the course of our lives, and love them very much. But it is to say that we must always give our whole hearts to the Lord and not just what is left over once everyone else has taken their piece.

Perhaps you feel like Peter, who answered in John 21:17, "Lord, You know I love You." And you are grieved that He is even asking you. Or maybe you are angry, thinking, *Why are you asking this of me, Lord? You know I love you, but don't you want me to be happy?* Or perhaps you are just flat-out confused—why would God bless you only to remove the blessing from your life at a later time?

God has bigger dreams for us than we have for ourselves.

The process of learning to love God more than these is one that refines us. It purifies us. We are fashioned in Christ's image as we walk through the experiences that require us to surrender our own dreams, desires, and plans and wholeheart-edly embrace God's will for our lives. His will is always so much greater and His plans are always so much bigger than we could ever dare to imagine. Yes, God has bigger dreams for us than we have for ourselves, and that is why we must learn to love Him more than *these,* and trust Him more than we trust our own hearts. In her bestselling book *Passion and Purity,* Elisabeth Elliot says this about surrender:

Think of [yourself] as an acorn. It is a marvelous little thing, a perfect shape, perfectly designed for its purpose, perfectly functional. Think of the grand glory of an oak tree. God's intention when He made the acorn was the oak tree. His intention for us is "...the measure of the stature of the fullness of Christ." Many deaths must go into our reaching that measure, many letting goes. When you look at the oak tree, you don't feel that "loss" of the acorn is a very great loss. The more you perceive God's purpose in your life, the less terrible will the losses seem.[1]

For every loss I have experienced in my life, for every dream I have ever been asked to surrender, God has always, without fail, given me beauty for my ashes as I have left the altar (Isaiah 61:3). Sometimes the beauty wasn't instant, and it took time for the dust to settle and the pain to subside. Other times it was an immediate exchange, and it happened so quickly that I almost didn't realize I ever had any ashes in the first place.

Living in the quick-fix world that we reside in today, I am sure most of us wish we could rush to the nearest "Beauty for

Ashes" line in the local department store and make a quick exchange of broken dreams for happily-ever-afters. Ideally, we will give up a friendship that is hindering us and have a new set of friends already lined up. We'll break up with a boyfriend we shouldn't be dating, and God will bring us someone else right away. We'll give and immediately get something in return.

But life doesn't work that way. We don't just wake up one morning and give it all up and love God as much as we possibly ever could. Although we may think we have reached the point where we love God above all else, we will always be able to love Him more. But will we always be able to love Him *more than* these?

That's a question that doesn't have a onetime answer. It must be answered over and over again every day for the rest of our lives, and it isn't answered with words. That question can only be answered with actions. So whether you are like Peter on the seashore, or like me knowing someone I had waited for and loved had to catch an airplane that would take him far away from me, the question is always asked for the same reason. The Lord asks us because He loves us.

The very fact that He is asking proves His love for us, and our answer proves our love for Him. What's your answer going to be right now?

"Daughter, do you love me more than *these?*"

FOR FURTHER THOUGHT:

1. List some things in your life that tend to rival your love for God at times.

2. How do you spend most of your free time? Do you give God as much time and attention as you give your friends and your hobbies?

3. Examine the passage in John 21. What do you think Jesus was asking Peter that day? Why do you think that?

4. What are some things you have had to remove from your life in the past because they were creating distance between you and God?

5. What is the one thing you absolutely would not want to give up for the Lord? What would you do if He asked you to do it?

LOVE IN ACTION:

Find the one thing in your life that rivals your love for the Lord the most, and consciously spend less time doing that thing (or being with that person) for one week. Spend the time reading God's Word, praying, or journaling your thoughts and prayers instead. Keep a daily log of how often you think about that person or thing, and how often you think about God. Be sure to note if you feel closer to God, and more refreshed and at peace since you are spending more time with Him. At the end of the week, carefully examine your log and see if the thing in question may be in danger of becoming an idol in your life.

Consciously restructure your schedule so you are spending more time with the Lord. Do you love Him more than *these*?

Notes

1. Elisabeth Elliot, *Passion and Purity* (Grand Rapids, MI: Fleming H. Revell, 1984), 163.

Epilogue

Hopefully, by now you have a clearer understanding of what true love is than you did when you first picked up this book. Love is a powerful thing. Song of Solomon 8:6 tells us it is as strong as death. It has the ability to change everything if we will let it.

If we love correctly—meaning, we love like Jesus loves—we will experience victory in our lives, and we will witness it in the lives of others. We will come to understand that love is not an emotion, but a choice—and perhaps the greatest choice we can ever make in our lives.

It is my earnest prayer that this book will be a great tool in your life as you seek to love the unlovable, create and keep the peace within the body of Christ, love at all times, be genuine in your attitudes and actions, love without fear, be firmly attached to the vine, lead others in love by example, and love God most of all.

If you ever find your love waning and your passion dimming, you need not look any further than the cross. There we will always find a reason to choose to love, and a solid and enduring example to follow. Remember, Jesus went to the cross for *you*. If you let that reality sink in and really penetrate you, loving that girl in your English class that is just plain mean will suddenly become a whole lot easier. In the end, none of us is really deserving of love and grace. But those of us who have lavishly received it should be willing to give it as well.

In your life you will be many things. You will be a teenager, a daughter, a friend, a student, and likely a high school graduate. You might also be an athlete, a musician, a writer, a dancer, or a wife and mother—among other things. All of those roles are both important and fun. But my hope is that your highest aspiration in life is to come out being a *girl who loves*.

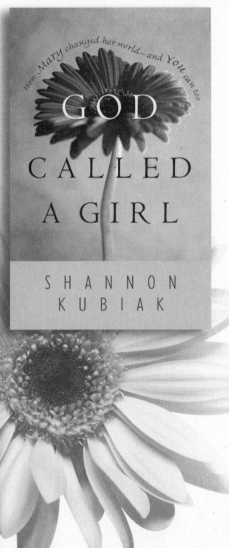